Federico Villanueva writes about on has
in the face of tragedy. It is often not ılly
or theologically explain why such eve ng
an answer as to why bad things happ ____ ui ueaiing with the
anguish, the pain, the anger, the questions, and the fears with which such
events overwhelm us.

Villanueva draws from the wealth of material in the Psalms. He warns
against a wrong type of spirituality of denying one's emotions and feelings,
and then forcibly trying to be happy and positive – somehow thinking
that this is what it means to always rejoice. Instead he allows people to
experience the depth of their God-given emotions and through that to find
healing and an awareness of God's presence. Besides the wealth of biblical
insights, this is a practical book filled with examples from Federico's life and
ministry. It is a resource for pastors as it addresses the various issues and
feelings that a tragedy evokes and then points to a Psalm that deals with it.
What then is most helpful is that he provides sermon outlines that a pastor
can use.

Rev Rupen Das

Research Professor,

Tyndale University College and Seminary, Toronto, Canada

This book is a gem, containing both rich and sensitive pastoral wisdom as
well as deep biblical reflection. Dr Villanueva brings his academic expertise
as well as his pastoral heart to make this an accessible and useful book that
pastors and preachers will benefit from enormously.

Rev Paul Barker

Assistant Bishop,

Anglican Diocese of Melbourne, Australia

Adjunct Old Testament Lecturer,

Myanmar Evangelical Graduate School of Theology, Myanmar

This is a vital book because, like its author, there are many in our churches around the world who feel "out of place in the gathering" for no reason other than their pain and sadness. Too often, our meetings inhabit a different world from the real one, a world of constant joy and easy life. But the Bible is not like that, as Rico's faithful expositions make so clear. While drawing on wisdom from modern psychology, the primary focus is on these ancient texts which were ahead of their time and as relevant today as ever. This is food for the mind and balm for the soul, and will restore much needed realism to many churches.

Mark Meynell

Associate Director - Europe & Caribbean,

Preaching Programme, Langham Partnership

It's OK to Be Not OK

Langham
PREACHING RESOURCES

It's OK to Be Not OK

Preaching the Lament Psalms

Federico G. Villanueva

Langham
PREACHING RESOURCES

Published 2017 by Langham Preaching Resources
An imprint of Langham Creative Projects

First published by OMF Literature Inc. in the Philippines in 2012
ISBN: 978-971-009-129-4

Langham Partnership
PO Box 296, Carlisle, Cumbria CA3 9WZ, UK
www.langham.org

Isbns:
978-1-90771-398-9 Print
978-1-78368-230-0 Mobi
978-1-78368-229-4 ePub
978-1-78368-231-7 PDF

British Library Cataloguing in Publication Data
A catalogue record for this book is available from the British Library

ISBN: 978-1-90771-398-9

Cover & Book Design: ProjectLuz.com

To my wife Rosemarie
and my children Emier and Faye

CONTENTS

Foreword

When the 2004 Tsunami in the Indian Ocean slammed into countries as far apart as Thailand, Indonesia, Sri Lanka and many islands in between, I was shocked with grief and moved to tears as I watched the news. I felt desperately grieved over the horrendous and sudden loss of life, especially among the poor who suffer so much already, and I felt angry with God. The following day was a Sunday and I went to church. But I could not sing the songs of praise that were included in the worship, because of the tears in my eyes and the lump in my throat. I could still worship God, but I could not say I was pleased to be there, and I could not understand his ways. I wanted to protest, not to praise.

At the same time, I could not join in the chorus of secular commentators who asked how Christians could continue to believe in God in the face of such tragedy, if he was presumed to exist and allow it. My faith in God, my love for him, my trust in his grace and provision – these things are lifetime realities and they cannot be shaken out of existence in the day of calamity. But they did not stop me from crying out to God with lament and protest.

That experience was part of the motivation that led me to write a book called *The God I Don't Understand* (which Dr Villanueva quotes in this book). Here is an extract from what I wrote there:

> When we run out of explanations [for suffering and disasters] or reject the ones we try, what are we to do? We lament and protest. We shout that it simply isn't fair. We cry out to God in anger. We tell him we can't understand and demand to know why he did not prevent it. Is it wrong to do this? Is it something that real believers shouldn't do, just like real men don't cry? Is it sinful to be angry with God? Again I turn to my Bible and find that the answer simply has to be No. Or at least, I find that God allows a great deal of anger to be expressed, even if, at times, he corrects it where it threatens to lead a person into sin or rebellion (as in the case of Jeremiah, 15:19–21).
>
> In the Bible there is plenty of lament, protest, anger and baffled questions. And the point we should notice (possibly to our surprise) is that it is all hurled at God, not by his enemies, but *by those who loved and trusted him most*. It seems, indeed,

that it is precisely those who have the closest relationship with God who feel most at liberty to pour out their pain and protest to God – without fear of reproach. Lament is not only allowed in the Bible – it is modelled for us in abundance. God seems to want to give us as many words with which to fill in our complaint forms as to write our thank you notes. Perhaps this is because whatever amount of lament the world causes us to express is a drop in the ocean compared to the grief in the heart of God himself at the totality of suffering that only God can comprehend.

Job gives us a whole bookful of such protest, and at the end, God declares that Job is more in the right than his friends who had so dogmatically given their "explanation" (and solution) to his suffering. Job himself is outrageously bold in his complaints to God and about God.

> "Then know that *God* has wronged me
> and drawn his net around me.
> Though I cry, 'Violence!' I get no response;
> though I call for help, there is no justice.
> *He* has blocked my way so I cannot pass;
> *he* has shrouded my paths in darkness." (Job 19:6–8; my italics)

Jeremiah (like Job) wishes he'd never been born, accuses God of cheating him, and pours out his pain to God (read especially Jer 15:10–21; 17:14–18; 20:7–18).

> "Why is my pain unending
> and my wound grievous and incurable?
> You [God] are to me like a deceptive brook,
> like a spring that fails." (Jer 15:18)

There is even a whole book in the Bible called Lamentations! Mind you it is written in the wake of calamity that is acknowledged to be the direct judgment of God, but even then the writer feels at liberty to pour out a mixture of protest and pleading to God. It is a powerfully pain-filled book constantly crying out to God against the terrible calamity that had befallen Jerusalem (Lam 2:11–12).

Psalm after psalm asks God questions like "How long, O LORD . . .?" and remonstrate over the suffering of the innocent and the apparent ease of the wicked (read, for example, Pss 10; 12; 13; 28; 30; 38; 56; 69; 88).

It surely cannot be accidental that in the divinely inspired book of Psalms there are more psalms of lament and anguish than of joy and thanksgiving. These are words that God has actually given us. God has allowed them a prominent place in his authorized songbook. We need both forms of worship in abundance as we live in this wonderful, terrible world.

I feel that the language of lament is seriously neglected in the church. Many Christians seem to feel that somehow it can't be right to complain to God in the context of corporate worship when we should all feel happy. There is an implicit pressure to stifle our real feelings because we are urged, by pious merchants of emotional denial, that we ought to have "faith" (as if the moaning psalmists didn't). So we end up giving external voice to pretended emotions we do not really feel, while hiding the real emotions we are struggling with deep inside. Going to worship can become an exercise in pretense and concealment – neither of which can possibly be conducive for a real encounter with God. So, in reaction to some appalling disaster or tragedy, rather than cry out our true feelings to God, we prefer other ways of responding to it.

"It's all part of God's curse on the earth."

"It's God's judgment."

"It's meant for a warning."

"It's ultimately for our own good."

"God is sovereign so that must make it all OK in the end."

But our suffering friends in the Bible didn't choose that way. They simply cry out in pain and protest against God – precisely because they know God. Their protest is born out of the jarring contrast between what they know and what they see. It is because they know God that they are so angry and upset. How can the God they know and love so much behave this way? They know that "the LORD is loving towards all he has made" (Ps 145:9, 13, 17). Why then does he allow things to happen that seem to indicate the opposite? They know the God who says "I take no pleasure in the death of the wicked" (Ezek 33:11). How then can he watch the deaths of hundreds of thousands whom Jesus would tell us are not necessarily any more sinful than the rest of us? They know the God whom Jesus says is there when even a sparrow falls to earth. Where is that God when the ocean swallows whole villages (and churches)?

Such radically inexplicable disasters fill biblical believers with desperate, passionate, concern for the very nature of God. So they cry out in vertigo above the chasm that seems to gape between the God they know and the world they live in. If God is supposed to be like that, how can the world be like this?

Lament is the voice of that pain, whether for oneself, for one's people, or simply for the mountain of suffering of humanity and creation itself. Lament is the voice of faith struggling to live with unanswered questions, and unexplained suffering.

God not only understands and accepts such lament; God has even given us words in the Bible to express it! An overflowing abundance of such words. Why then are we so reluctant to give voice to what God allows in his Word, using the words of those who wrote them for us out of their own suffering faith?

In the wake of something like the tsunami, then, I am not ashamed to feel and express my anger and lament. I am not embarrassed to shed tears watching the news or worshipping in church after such terrible tragedies have struck again. I tell the God I know and love and trust, but don't always understand, that I just can't get my head around the pain of seeing such unspeakable destruction and death. I will cry out on behalf of the wretched of the earth, "Why those poor people, Lord, yet again? Haven't they suffered enough of this world's gross unfairness already?"

I'm not waiting for an answer, but I will not spare God the question. For am I not also made in God's image? Has God not planted a pale reflection of his own infinite compassion and mercy in the tiny finite cage of my heart too? If there is joy in heaven over one sinner that repents, are there not also tears in heaven over thousands swept to their death?[1]

---

1. Taken from Christopher J. H. Wright, *The God I Don't Understand: Reflections on Tough Questions of Faith* (Grand Rapids, MI: Zondervan, 2008), 50–53. Copyright © 2008 by Christopher J. H. Wright. Used by permission of Zondervan. www.zondervan.com.

Having written all that, it is no surprise that I warmly welcome and strongly recommend this book by Rico Villanueva. I got to know Rico as a Langham Scholar in the UK, doing his doctorate study on the Psalms. He pays attention to what so many pastors and preachers ignore (and in effect implicitly deny) – the songs of lament and protest in the Bible – and helps us to relate them to the broken and painful realities of our own lives. May this book bring encouragement and reassurance to many. May it protect us from the lies of those who tell us that simply having faith makes everything in life OK. And may it renew our love for God and our trust in him in the midst of those times when things go horribly wrong.

Rev Chris Wright, PhD

International Ministries Director, Langham Partnership

Preface

Japanese theologian Kazoh Kitamori said that in order to write about suffering, one has to experience it first. But then he asks, how can one write about suffering when one is going through a hard time while writing? Among many other things, writing requires resources, support, and concentration. So how can one write during times of suffering, when life is hard? The answer, according to Kitamori, is God's mercy.

Reflecting on everything I have gone through, some of which I share in this book, I can say that it is only by God's mercy that I have been able to finish this project. And God's mercy is not some abstract idea, but is concretely expressed through the people, situations, organizations, and resources God brings our way to accomplish the task he has entrusted to us.

I thank God for his mercy, expressed through the people he used to enable me to accomplish the task. I extend my thanks to these people as well, foremost of whom are my family: my wife Rosemarie, for simply believing in me, encouraging me, and accepting me even when I am not OK; my daughter Faye for reading portions of the book and telling me afterwards how she felt "accepted"; my son Emier, who joined the whole family in praying for this book; my parents Bishop Butch and Melita Villanueva, for their moral support and prayers; and my brothers Demo and Jojo, cousin Boyet and his wife Carla (who read the manuscript) for encouraging me to pursue this book.

I thank Dr Christopher Wright for writing the foreword and Pieter Kwant who suggested the title, "It's OK to Be Not OK" and who told me he wanted to see this book. The present book was earlier published by OMF Literature. I have revised the book so that it will not only be for general readership but also for use in Langham Preaching Resources (LPR). I thank Dr Paul Windsor, director of Langham Preaching, for recommending this book for inclusion in the LPR imprint. Isobel Stevenson, who read early drafts of this book, has been a great help in reshaping the book to fit the imprint.

My thanks also to my friends, colleagues, and co-workers in the ministry who journeyed with me as I wrote this book: Dr Fernando and Dr Teresa Lua, Pastor Eric Obado, Dr Edwin Perona, Dr Hannah Haskel, Dr Alwin De Leon, Rev Benjie De Jesus, Dr Wil Hernandez, and my RootWord writer's group, with Dr Mona Bias and Dr Rod Santos.

To the churches and communities where I had the opportunity to share some of the ideas found in this book through preaching and teaching – Life Gospel Church (LGC) where the impetus for this book started, Proclaim Christ until He Comes Church (especially the church's Bible Institute), St Mary Magdalene Church (Bristol, England), Jesus Cares Fellowship (Bristol, England), Christian Alliance Fellowship East (especially my Wednesday group), Capital City Alliance Church (CCAC), Faith, Hope, and Love Prayer Institute and Seminary, United Evangelical Churches of the Philippines (UECP), Alliance Graduate School (AGS), Society of Divine Word, Tagaytay, and Loyola School of Theology (Ateneo de Manila) – thank you for the privilege of learning and sharing with you.

And to Langham Partnership whose writer's grant enabled me to have some time away to focus on writing.

I give God all the praise and glory for his mercy and grace!

Rico Villanueva

Cainta, Rizal

September 2016

1

Introduction

"The water has already reached the second floor!"

Jojo is my youngest brother. He and his wife and their two daughters – a seven-year-old and a baby – were trapped by floodwaters entering their house. I didn't know how to respond to his call. My family and I were in the same predicament and had been trying to save what we could. We had carried most of our belongings to the second floor of our home – including our refrigerator and everything else we could lift. We too were panicking. The water had not yet reached our second floor, but it was rising fast. The rain had been going on all night and had not stopped. There was no way I could help Jojo and his family.

Fortunately, Jojo came up with a plan. He broke a window, tied some rope around the grilles and fashioned a fragile bridge to a neighboring house. Then he and his wife carried their children across that rope. The ordeal was frightening. The water far below was deep, and the current was strong. If they fell, they would die.

Houses and cars in the vicinity were being carried away by the raging waters. A news camera captured harrowing footage of two boys, no more than ten years old, clinging to the branch of a broken tree. When the strength of the flood broke their grip on the branch, the current swept them away. Their hands were clasped in a position of prayer as the waters carried them to their deaths. I know of a mother who watched all of this happen on TV. She looked at her children, two boys about the same age as the ones who had just perished. *Why*, she wondered, *did those boys die when they were praying, while my children were spared?*

All this took place on a Saturday in 2009 as Typhoon Ondoy destroyed houses, villages, and countless lives. Even those who were not directly harmed were deeply affected. I myself began to suffer panic attacks whenever there was strong rain.

The next day, Sunday, none of us were able to go to church – many churches were under water. In our village, it took several more days for the floodwaters to recede. In other places, it was months before the water dried up. But one week after the typhoon, the very first Sunday we were able to go to church, I preached at the Sunday service in a small church. To my amazement, the worship leader spoke as if everything was normal. He didn't even mention Ondoy. We sang three hymns, none of which related in any way to what we had just experienced. I remember holding the hymnal in my hands, reading the praise hymn the audience was singing, and – I could not sing the words. The prayers that day did not mention the tragedy we had just endured. I asked myself, *Why is there nothing in our worship about what we have experienced?*

"We only sing happy songs"

I had been asking myself this question for a long time. When I was pastoring a church in Manila, we would gather in church Sunday after Sunday and sing songs to the Lord – mostly praise songs. From time to time, some terrible difficulty would strike our members – sickness, some serious problem, some form of suffering – and yet our songs remained the same.

There was a mismatch between what we were singing and what we were experiencing. Most of the songs we sing in church come from the West. Many of them are good songs, but many also do not fit in with our experiences as a suffering people. They tend to present life as always bright, always beautiful. Even some of our Tagalog songs are no different. One of the most well-known Tagalog songs declares: "*Ang buhay ng Kristiyano ay masayang tunay . . . laging masayang tunay*" [The Christian life is a happy life indeed . . . happy all the time]. Another Tagalog song tells us: "*Kasama natin ang Diyos, di ako matatakot . . . Dumaan man ako sa ilog, di ako malulunod*" [God is with us, I will not be afraid . . . Even if I pass through rivers, I will not drown]. Even when our homes and villages are flooded, we continue to sing happy songs!

Positive testimonies only?

You will notice the same emphasis when you listen to what's called "sharing" or testimonies in church gatherings. I once attended a gathering of pastors in

Manila, where the pastor-emcee started the program by saying, *"Bawal ang nakasimangot dito!"* [A frowning face is prohibited here!]. Maybe he was only joking, but his words reflect the general view that when you are in church or at Christian gatherings, you are supposed to be OK. But I was not feeling OK emotionally. And on top of that, I now felt out of place in the gathering.

Later, when I spoke to the person responsible for pastoral care in a certain denomination, he confirmed that my experience was not an isolated one. He related that at a district pastors' gathering the leader started by saying, "It's testimony time. We want to hear your praises. Please don't talk about your problems because it will not bless anyone."[1] Many of the pastors had come to this gathering to unload their burdens, but they were prevented from doing so. That is why many pastors choose not attend such meetings. Pastors' gatherings can also, at times, be overly focused on accomplishments. From my experience, the number one thing that is talked about is how their church is growing and how many members they have. I once asked a pastor-friend whom I had not seen for a long time, "How are *you*?" He responded by telling me about his *church*, how it was doing well and growing.

Unfortunately, what happens in church leaders' gatherings spills over into the church. Observe how sharing or testimony times go in our churches. Most, if not all of them, revolve around positive things, resolved problems, and answered prayers. When was the last time you listened to someone standing in front of the church, sharing a painful struggle they were going through, and then just stopping there? When was the last time you saw someone cry in front of the church because he or she could no longer carry on?

We make sure our worship gatherings are full of celebration, like a fiesta. Our songs are mostly upbeat, and our worship teams make a point of always ending on a high note. One seminary professor in the USA, whose wife had divorced him, commented that during the five years of pain and suffering he endured, the only part of the worship service that was meaningful and helpful to him was the assistant pastor's five-minute prayer for suffering people. The rest of the service – the singing, the sermon, and everything else – was for happy people. I'm afraid we can say the same thing for many evangelical churches in our country. Even when we share our problems during testimony times, we usually end with statements like: "But I know everything will be OK" or "But I know God has a purpose." Although these statements are true,

---

1. Personal correspondence with Rev Narciso V. Castro, Jr, National Minister for Pastoral Care of the Alliance of Bible Christian Churches of the Philippines.

I wonder if those who utter them only do so in order to cover up or deny their pain and uncertainty. Or maybe, they just feel that they must follow a "script."

Scott Ellington once conducted a study of how testimonies were done in a certain group of churches. What he found was revealing. He discovered that testimonies were no longer spontaneous; they were being screened by the leaders before they were made in public. The leaders wanted to make sure that whatever was publicly shared would build up the faith.[2] An unanswered prayer would not qualify as a "testimony."

But if the only sharing and testimonies we hear are about answered prayers and victorious experiences, then we leave out the experience of quite a number of those in the church. While some can testify about the great things the Lord has been doing in their lives, others find it hard to identify with what they are saying. Some may, in fact, wonder why the prayers of those testifying have been answered while their own prayers have not. In the same manner, when our congregations sing victory songs, some of us may have a hard time singing along. There is a Tagalog song: *"Kahit may problema at wala kang pera, di ba't laging masaya?"* [Even if there is a problem and you don't have money, aren't we always happy?] But tell this to the wife who is worried every time the electric bill comes. Tell this to the father who was forced to take his daughter out of college because he no longer has the money for tuition. We sing *"Kasama natin ang Diyos . . . di ako malulunod"* [God is with me . . . I will not drown]. But how can the loved ones of those who were swept away by the tsunami sing that song? We sing, *"Kasama natin ang Diyos . . . di ako masusunog"* [God is with me . . . I will not be burned]. How can one of my church members whose house burned down identify with that? How can families relate to that when earthquakes in New Zealand and Japan in 2011 killed their loved ones and shattered their lives? How can the father who lost all his family members during Typhoon Sendong, which killed more than 5,000 people, even think of singing such a song?

---

2. Scott A. Ellington, "The Costly Loss of Testimony," *Journal of Pentecostal Theology* 16 (2000): 48–59.

Deleting the negative in church

Sadly, I feel that for the most part we have successfully deleted what many consider the "negative."[3] There is no room for negative emotions like despair, sadness, loneliness, fear and anger; no room for negative actions like struggling, mourning, weeping, crying and questioning God; no room for negative situations like failure, accidents and calamities. Generally today,

- it's not OK to be down
- it's not OK to be sad
- it's not OK to cry
- it's not OK to be afraid
- it's not OK to struggle
- it's not OK to be angry
- it's not OK to question God
- it's not OK to fail

Speaking of his own experiences in Singapore, Gordon Wong, an Old Testament scholar and pastor, writes: "Our churches emphasize prayer and praise to God. But we almost always think that the only prayers acceptable to God are words of praise and thanksgiving."[4] He points out the absence of such prayers in the lament psalms and Habakkuk:

> Many churches today have lost this major dimension of prayer and worship. We emphasize thanksgiving so much that we give the impression that God can only be worshipped by the happy soul, or only by the person who feels full of praise. Many of our comments at worship are aimed at urging the worshipper to feel in a "correct" way, a good way, a positive and joyful way. We may even say things like, "You can't truly worship God if you are worried about your troubles. Leave aside your problems right now. We are in the house of God. Don't be distracted by the cares of this world. Just focus on God and praise his name."[5]

---

3. I am calling them "negative" here, but not because I consider them negative. As I will show in this book, emotions which people usually consider negative, like anger, can actually be positive emotions. But here I retain the word "negative" because that is how many people today view these emotions.

4. Gordon Wong, *God, Why?: Habakkuk's Struggle with Faith in a World Out of Control* (Singapore: Armour, 2007), 7.

5. Ibid.

Denise Ackermann, a South African Christian leader, has observed something similar:

> Acts of lamentation have disappeared from our liturgies in our churches. Keening [wailing in grief] bodies addressing God directly, calling God to account for the intractability of suffering, are deemed to be liturgically inappropriate in mainline Christianity in my country.[6]

A look at the worship books of most mainline denominations reveals that "psalms of lament are poorly represented . . . With notable exceptions, it would appear that prayer and worship in many Christian congregations fail to make room for the experiences of lament, protest, and remonstration with God."[7]

Ill-prepared to face tragedy

Because there is no room in the church for our negative experiences, we do not know how to respond when tragic events occur. John Swinton relates his own experience in Ireland after the Omagh bombing, which killed twenty-eight people and left about two hundred others wounded and maimed. Shortly after the bombing, Swinton attended church and observed (as I did after Typhoon Ondoy devastated Manila) that there was no mention of the tragedy in the entire worship service.

> Something was seriously wrong with our church, and despite the fact that I had been attending there for ten years, I had never noticed it. It seemed that we had no capacity for dealing with sadness. As I reflected on the way in which my church worshipped, its emphasis, its tone, its expectations, its expressed hopes, I suddenly understood clearly that *there was no room in our liturgy and worship for sadness, brokenness, and questioning.* We had much space for love, joy, praise, and supplication, but it seemed that we viewed the acknowledgement of sadness and

---

6. Denise Ackermann, "'A Voice Was Heard in Ramah': A Feminist Theology of Praxis for Healing in South Africa," in *Liberating Faith Practices: Feminist Practical Theologies in Context,* eds. Denise Ackermann and Riet Bons-Storm (Leuven: Peeters, 1998), 96; cited in John Swinton, *Raging with Compassion: Pastoral Responses to the Problem of Evil* (Grand Rapids, MI: Eerdmans, 2007), 115.

7. K. D. Billman and D. L. Migliore, *Rachel's Cry: Prayer of Lament and the Rebirth of Hope* (Portland, OR: Wipf & Stock, 1999), 13.

the tragic brokenness of our world as almost tantamount to faithlessness. As a result, *when tragedy hit . . . we had no idea what to do with it or how to formulate our concerns. Because we had not consistently practiced the art of recognizing, accepting, and expressing sadness, we had not developed the capacity to deal with tragedy* . . . In the face of evil and suffering, we sang cheerful songs and expressed happy thoughts rather than weeping with the wounded and lamenting with the Sovereign God.[8]

Denying their true feelings

Because there is no room in the church for our negative experiences, not only are we ill-prepared when tragedy strikes, but people also learn to deny their true feelings. Since there is no room for their negative experiences, they learn to hide these. They feel obliged to create their own "virtual identity" – the "always OK" image. Old Testament scholar and Christian leader Chris Wright remarks:

> There is an implicit pressure to stifle our real feelings because we are urged, by pious merchants of emotional denial, that we ought to have "faith" . . . So we end up giving external voice to pretended emotions we do not really feel, while hiding the real emotions we are struggling with deep inside.[9]

So what do we do? How do we address the church's failure to make room for our negative experiences?

---

8. Swinton, *Raging with Compassion*, 92–93, emphasis mine.
9. Wright, *The God I Don't Understand*, 52.

2

Learning from the Lament Psalms

Sunday after Sunday, I watched the growing rift between what we were experiencing and what we were declaring through our songs and testimonies. So I began looking for guidance to address this. What I found was there were laments throughout the Old Testament (e.g. Isa 63:7–64:11; the book of Lamentations). But laments were particularly concentrated in the book of Psalms, which is full of songs and prayers arising out of the people's experience of suffering. There I found the voice I was looking for, the voice that comes from the depths. "Out of the depths I cry to you, O LORD" (Ps 130:1).

What are the lament psalms?

The authors of the lament psalms are not simply complaining or moaning about things like being stuck in a traffic jam. They arise from serious, persistent, can't-get-away-from it experiences of despair. Some are triggered by national crises like a crop failure or being defeated in a war (Ps 44) and may seem to be written for the king, who refers to himself as "I" when speaking on behalf of his suffering people. Others speak of more personal crises like a prolonged illness (Ps 6), depression (Ps 13:2), or betrayal by someone very close to you (Ps 55:12–14).[1]

---

1. In his book *Psalms: Reading and Studying the Book of Praises* (Peabody, MA: Hendrickson, 1990; 23) W. H. Bellinger divides the lament psalms up as follows:

Individual lament psalms: 3, 4, 5, 6, 7, 9–10, 11, 13, 16, 17, 22, 25, 26, 27, 28, 31, 35, 36, 38, 39, 40, 42–43, 51, 52, 54, 55, 56, 57, 59, 61, 62, 63, 64, 69, 70, 71, 77, 86, 88, 94, 102, 109, 120, 130, 140, 141, 143

Communal lament psalms: 12, 14, 44, 53, 58, 60, 74, 79, 80, 83, 85, 90, 106, 108, 123, 126, 137

It is important to note that all of these laments, the communal and the personal, are part of the book of Psalms, which functioned rather like the hymnbook used in worship in the temple in Jerusalem. This means that even the personal laments were not purely personal but were meant to be used by the community. The writers lamented before God in the context of the community, and the community wrote down and used their laments.

The people who wrote the lament psalms did not keep silent about what they were feeling or experiencing. They put their experience down in poetry and music. While we no longer have access to the original music of these psalms, the poetic words remain, along with the emotion that went with them. In these laments we hear the people's agony. We feel their pain. We are privileged to see the struggles, sufferings, and darkness Old Testament believers went through. We are invited to walk with them "through the valley of the shadow of death" as they take us to a road that leads to light. Their laments make us feel we are not alone. They offer us words that we can use on our own journey which is also marked by pain and suffering.

Most important of all, the lament psalms open the way to God. They are not just empty words uttered to no one. God's people have someone to whom they can direct their laments. In fact, a lament is a type of prayer. That is what distinguishes biblical lament from many modern laments, which merely complain about life in general, the government, corruption, and so on. The laments we find in the Psalms are not just complaints; they are prayers, honest prayers.

What makes the lament psalms particularly powerful is that they are both prayer and Word. The lament psalms have been included in our Bible, and therefore bear an important message for us today. They invite us to bring all our negative emotions and failures to God. Using their very words, we can struggle, weep, and even express our questions to God.

Why preach on the lament psalms?

As we saw in the previous chapter, the strong emphasis on the positive and on victory in some of our churches and communities means that our negative experiences are drowned out by the noise of praise. But our negative experiences are real, and they have a place in the Bible. We as pastors have a responsibility to help our people understand this by preaching on the psalms of lament. By doing this, we will

- *create space for our negative experiences within the worshipping community.* We need the lament psalms to give voice to our negative experiences. These psalms tell us it's OK to be not OK. There is room for our sadness, depression, anger, questions, and struggles. We do not have to deny them; they are part of our spirituality and of our whole walk with God. By acknowledging them and bringing them to God in the way that the lament psalms do, we make our negative experiences occasions for growth and intimacy with God.
- *challenge people to confront their sufferings and struggles.* None of us want pain or suffering. We would rather deny or ignore them. But we also know that none of us are immune to suffering. None of us go through life unscathed. We will all have days when we just don't want to get up anymore. Some of us have to go to church on Sundays when we are not feeling well or are struggling inside. Without the lament, there might not be any opportunity to address what we are going through. Most parts of the worship service – the songs, the sermon, etc. – are for people who are OK. By bringing on board the lament psalms, we make sure our negative experiences are given the attention they need. This may cause unease for some. Who wants to admit that they are not OK? But we cannot move towards restoration until we face up to our true situation.
- *invite people to come to God and pour out their hearts to him.* The lament psalms provide us with the words we can utter to God. There are times when we just don't know what to say. The beauty of the lament psalms is that they express for us what we are going through. All the emotions we go through are found in the Psalms, including the negative ones. And since the lament psalms are prayers, they become vehicles for pouring out our own personal cries and petitions to God. One of the best ways of preaching lament is by inviting the congregation to pray the words of the lament at the end.

I put the above ideas into practice by starting to teach and preach on the lament psalms whenever appropriate. I would teach about lament in our prayer meetings, preach about it during Holy Week and on other occasions. After two years of doing this, I started to see some fruit. One time, we had what I would call a modern experience of communal lament. That Sunday morning, after the worship service ended and everyone was about to leave, one of the members – a mother – came forward and started sharing her struggles. She was crying. The members who were leaving returned and listened to her. This was not the typical sharing of "I have a problem, but . . ." The mother was actually sharing a lament with the congregation. I slowly came forward from the back of the church. After she had finished sharing, and while she was still sobbing, I led the congregation in a prayer of lament. I said how terrible we felt about what had happened to her. "We feel like hell," I said. I did not end on a positive note. I ended my words just like that. But when I opened my eyes, I saw many of our members in tears. I sensed in them a relief and a feeling of liberation. It's OK to be not OK in the church.

That is the message of this book. If I may summarize the message of the lament psalms, it is this:

"It's OK to be Not OK"
- It's OK to be down
- It's OK to be sad
- It's OK to be afraid
- It's OK to be angry
- It's OK to struggle
- It's OK to weep
- It's OK to question God
- It's OK to fail

I hope that this book will help you to understand how we can use these psalms in our churches and communities. We will learn to appreciate them as *poetry*, which vividly expresses our human sorrows, as *pointers* to God, as they teach us a theology of suffering, and as *prayers*, with which we can identify and which we can make our own when words fail us because of our grief.

How do we preach on a lament psalm?

It is still far too early in the book to give you detailed instructions on how to go about preparing a sermon on a psalm of lament. There will be examples of that as you go along, and some detailed examples are worked out in the Appendix. At this stage, all I want to do is draw your attention to four key steps that will help you discern God's message for you and for those to whom you preach.

1. Pay attention to the movement between lament and praise in these psalms.

2. Identify the types of suffering depicted in each psalm.

3. Discern what messages about God, the life of faith and reality in general we can derive from the depictions of sufferings.

4. Participate in each lament psalm by actually praying the words of the psalm, experiencing the movements between lament and praise yourself, and bringing your own experiences and that of others to God as you identify with the sufferings depicted in the psalm.

Each chapter in this book ends with an invitation to you to spend time encountering one of the psalms of lament. May God speak to you, and through you to his people, as you meditate on what it means for us to lament together.

3

It's OK to Be Down

A dear sister in the Lord once told me: "I need to be stronger more than ever. For is it not during our times of trials that we should all the more show our faith in the Lord?" This sister had been going through one of the most difficult times in her life. She had discovered that her boyfriend of a number of years was already married. I was saddened to hear this news because the last time we talked I had thought they were planning to get married. In spite of the problem, she had kept on with the relationship for some time, hoping things would work out. But nothing happened, and so she was forced to break off the relationship. She was close to fifty years old, uncertain of ever getting married. Looking into her eyes, I saw loneliness and deep sadness. She wanted to be strong. She did not want to admit to being down. Yet she was also asking me: "Is this the way it's supposed to be? Are we not allowed to be down, even when we are going through some really difficult situation?"

What I want to tell her is what I want to tell you in this chapter: It's OK to be down. But first, what do we mean by the word "down"? I think the song "Precious Lord" best describes what we mean by "being down." This song was composed by Thomas A. Dorsey in response to the death of his wife in childbirth. The baby had also died. Some lines from the song specifically depict what we mean by the word "down":

"I am tired, I am weak, I am worn"

"When my way grows drear"

"When my life is almost gone"

"When the darkness appears and the night draws near"

"And the day is past and gone"[1]

You may be able to identify with some of those words and the feelings reflected in them. In the Bible we find that even people of great faith, those who were closest to God, experienced what it means to be down. I can almost hear Moses crying out, "I am tired, I am weak, I am worn" because of the constant complaints and grumbling of the Israelites. It had all become too much for Moses, and so he actually prayed for God to take him away:

> I cannot carry all these people by myself; the burden is too heavy for me. If this is how you are going to treat me, put me to death right now – if I have found favor in your eyes – and do not let me face my own ruin. (Num 11:14–15)

Elijah could easily sing the words, "When my life is almost gone." He too wished he were dead. And this happened right after one of the most amazing events in his ministry as a prophet – winning the competition against the prophets of Baal. But as 1 Kings 19:4 tells us:

> While he himself went a day's journey into the desert. He came to a broom tree, sat down under it and prayed that he might die. "I have had enough, Lord," he said. "Take my life; I am no better than my ancestors."

The author of Psalm 88 knows very well the darkness spoken about in the line "When the darkness appears and the night draws near." He says:

> You have taken my companions and loved ones from me; the darkness is my closest friend. (Ps 88:18)

And how can we miss Jeremiah, known as the "weeping prophet"? Listen to his words:

> Oh, that my head were a spring of water and my eyes a fountain of tears! I would weep day and night for the slain of my people. (Jer 9:1)

This short list of people in the Bible shows that being down is not something only weaklings experience. Even the best of God's people can be down.

---

1. Thomas A. Dorsey, "Precious Lord, Take My Hand," copyright © 1938 Hill & Range Songs, Inc. Copyright Renewed, assigned to Unichappell Music, Inc. (Rightsong Music, Publisher). Used by permission of Hal Leonard Corporation.

Some of the psalms also deal with the experience of someone who is very close to God but feels down. Look at Psalms 42/43, which begins with the familiar words, "As the deer pants for streams of water, so my soul pants for you, O God" (Ps 42:1).[2] Like Moses, Elijah, and Jeremiah, this psalmist is someone who is close to God. In verse 1 he compares his longing for God with that of a deer looking for water. Israel is a dry country, and when it does rain, the water quickly flows away. Water comes and goes quickly, and there is little, if any, to be found when the poor deer looks for it. The psalmist watches the deer desperately searching for water, water that has already gone, and he says to God: "God, like that deer, bound to die if it cannot find water, so I am dying for you."

And yet this person who longs so deeply for God with all his being tells us that instead of finding God, all he has are tears:

My tears have been my food day and night, while men say to me
all day long, "Where is your God?" (v. 3)

The only "water" he is finding is the water of his own tears. His longing for God did not bring him peace and joy, or even a release from whatever emotional turmoil he was experiencing. Instead, it aggravated his situation.

The psalmist does not easily give up, however. He encourages himself; he actually talks to his soul:

Why are you downcast, O my soul? . . . Put your hope in God.
(v. 5)

He rouses his soul and asks himself, "Why are you down? That's not where you're supposed to be." Maybe he has been told that people who are close to God should always be OK. And so he commands his soul to trust in God:

Put your hope in God, for I will yet praise him, my Savior and
my God. (vv. 5–6a)

But in spite of his initial attempts he confesses,

My soul is downcast within me. (v. 6a)

I find this confession brave. To admit that you are not OK, to admit that you are down, is a remarkable feat. When all the voices you hear, including your own, are telling you, "Keep trusting in God," or "Don't give up," this psalmist is telling us: "You know what? I've struggled and tried to keep my

---

2. Psalm 42 and 43 actually form one psalm, as indicated by the presence of the same refrain in both chapters (42:5, 11; 43:5) and the absence of a superscription in Psalm 43.

soul from being in despair. I've even tried remembering those commands and encouraging words to 'put your hope in God.' But to be honest about it, I'm still down."

He tries to encourage himself further by remembering the Lord –

> Therefore I will remember you from the land of the Jordan, the heights of Hermon – from Mount Mizar. (v. 6)

– but the more he tries, the more he feels down. He tells the Lord:

> All your waves and breakers have swept over me. (v. 7)

Like the two boys who were swept away by the waters of Ondoy (see Introduction), the psalmist is drowning; he feels his life ebbing away.

Three times he repeats the words, "Why are you downcast, O my soul? Put your hope in God" (Pss 42:5, 11; 43:5). This demonstrates the psalmist's perseverance. At the same time, it tells us that even a life lived in close fellowship with God, the life of someone who deeply longs for God, is not immune to the experience of despair.

Jesus himself became downcast. Matthew quotes Jesus's words:

> My soul is overwhelmed with sorrow to the point of death. (Matt 26:38)

Here the Greek word translated as "overwhelmed with sorrow" is the same word we find used to translate "downcast" in the ancient Greek translation of Psalm 42:5.[3] What Jesus experienced in the Garden of Gethsemane was not merely being down. He was not just sorrowful; he was "very sorrowful." Matthew says that he was sorrowful "to the point of death" (Matt 26:38). Luke tells us that Jesus's agony was such that "*his sweat was like drops of blood falling to the ground*" (Luke 22:44, emphasis mine).

Like Moses, the psalmist, and others, Jesus experienced what it means to be downcast. But what is even more remarkable is that he told his disciples about it. Jesus did not think it improper to admit, "My soul is overwhelmed with sorrow to the point of death." The people I mentioned earlier – Moses, Elijah, Jeremiah, and the psalmist – all experienced despair and expressed this to God. Jesus, however, confessed his feeling of being down to his disciples.

If you are a pastor, try telling leaders in your church today, "I am down, really down." You might lose your job! One of my students told me that if

---

3. The Greek word used is *perilupos*.

he shows he is weak and admits to having negative emotions, he will not be promoted to a leadership position.

Isn't that sad? We cannot even be honest about what we are going through, especially if it involves some negative emotion like despair, depression or deep sadness. It seems that we have come to a point in our Christian life as a community when we can no longer show that we are down. We are always expected to be OK. But the question is: *Are we really OK?* Are there not times in our lives when we just want to quit? Are there not nights and days when, like the psalmist, "our tears have been our food"?

In her book, *Pilgrim at Tinker Creek*, Annie Dillard describes various animals that she had been closely observing. She saw that almost all the adult spiders "tended to be missing a leg or two." She writes:

> I think of all the butterflies I have seen whose torn hind wings bore the jagged marks of birds' bills. There were four or five tiger swallowtails missing one of their tails, and a fritillary missing two-thirds of a hind wing. The birds, too, who make up the bulk of my list, always seem to have been snatched at from behind, except for the killdeer I saw just yesterday, who was missing all of its toes . . . Once I saw a swallowtailed sparrow, who on second look proved to be a sparrow from whose tail the central wedge of feathers had been torn. I've seen a completely tailless sparrow, a tailless robin.[4]

I look at people around me in the church and workplace and wonder: Aren't we all like those broken little creatures in Annie Dillard's book? How many of us have scars, scratches on our back, deep wounds, swelling fingers, broken legs, and aching arms, still barely escaping life's cruel realities? I look at myself and wonder at how I have managed all these years to continue. I have survived challenges in my ministry, in my studies, and in my marriage. I haven't emerged unscathed. While in the midst of these challenges, I felt, at times, as if I had been asked to run or walk without feet, to carry a load with my back broken, and to hold a heavy burden with feeble hands. Many of us are broken, but we don't want to show it. We are afraid we might be rejected by others. We have been taught it's not OK to be down.

But as we have seen in the lives of God's people, including that of Jesus himself, even those who are closest to God can be down. The experience of

---

4. Annie Dillard, *Pilgrim at Tinker Creek* (New York: Harper and Row, 1974), 235–236.

the psalmist in particular teaches us that being down is not necessarily a sign of weak faith or that we live far from God. On the contrary, it can be an indication of a growing and deepening relationship with God. As the Spanish scholar Alonso Schökel tells us, one way of knowing we have experienced God's presence is how we sense his absence:

> The manner of God's presence is awareness of his absence. Absence which is not noticed nor deeply felt is a simple absence which causes no grief. But absence which is felt is a means of being present in the consciousness, bringing anxiety and grief . . . God communicates most intensely by creating an awareness of his absence.[5]

Somebody once asked me how it feels to be away from my family for a week. I told him, "I miss them painfully."

We tend to think that when we are in the presence of God, it's all peace and joy and serenity. One of the songs we sing goes like this:

> In your presence, there is comfort,
> In your presence, there is peace.[6]

But it's not actually always like that, according to spiritual writer Thomas Merton. He likens the Christian life to a desert:

> Let us never forget that the ordinary way to contemplation lies through a desert without trees and without beauty and without water. The spirit enters a wilderness and travels blindly in directions that seem to lead away from vision, away from God, away from all fulfillment and joy. It may become almost impossible to believe that this road goes anywhere at all except to a desolation full of dry bones – the ruin of all our hopes and good intentions.[7]

The experiences of the psalmist and of God's people in the Bible demonstrate that a close walk with God is not just all about what we consider "positive" emotions. One spiritual writer, St John of the Cross, even wrote about "the dark night of the soul." Other Christians have testified of their own

---

5. Alonso Schökel, "The Poetic Structure of Psalm 42–43," *JSOT* 1 (1976): 8–9.

6. By Sandi Patti, http://www.lyricstime.com/sandi-patty-in-his-presence-lyrics.html, accessed 17 Feb 2012.

7. Thomas Merton, *New Seeds of Contemplation* (New York: New Directions Books, 1972, 1961), 156, emphasis mine.

experiences of this "dark night." The German theologian Dietrich Bonhoeffer, who was ordered hanged by Hitler, writes: "This longing to know God's judgments, cost what it may, is not a power of the soul; on the contrary, it is the soul's death . . . When this longing for God comes over us, then the soul suffers torment, then it is prostrate, then its fine structure is consumed."

Mother Teresa, whose smile captivated the sick and dying in Calcutta and the world over, admits: "There is so much contradiction in my soul. Such deep longing for God – so deep that it is painful." I quote these words from the book *Mother Teresa: Come Be My Light*, which contains some of her confessions, published after she died.[8] In the same book, Mother Teresa asks for prayer from one of her confessors. Her request for prayer resembles the psalmist's experience in Psalm 42/43. She says, "Please pray for me – the longing for God is terribly painful and yet the darkness is becoming greater."

Do you feel down today? The good news is that you don't have to pretend you are not. Like the psalmist, you can actually say, "My soul is downcast." It's OK to be down. It's OK to admit we are down. Most importantly, it's OK to come to God when we are down – especially when we are down. For as we have learned:

- Even God's people, including Jesus, experienced being down.
- They were not afraid or ashamed to acknowledge before God or before people that they felt down.[9]
- Being down is not always an indication that something is wrong with us. Psalm 42/43 tells us that being down can be an indication of growing intimacy with God.
- Most important of all, we can come to God even when we are down. In fact, we should come to God especially when we are down.

However, just because "it's OK to be down" does not mean we should stay down. As we go through the different seasons of life, so our responses should change. The problem is that we often think that negative experiences like being down are unacceptable in the life of Christian faith.

Related to this is another problem: we usually have only one response to all of life's situations. We'll talk about this in the next chapter.

---

8. Brian Kolodiejchuk, ed., *Mother Teresa: Come Be My Light* (New York: Doubleday, 2007).

9. Of course, I do not mean to suggest here that we broadcast to everyone that we are down. Jesus opened up his heart to those closest to him. The problem today is that sometimes it's hard for us to share our true feelings even with those closest to us, for fear they may not understand.

Encountering a psalm

Read Psalm 42/43.

- The psalmist likens his longing for God to that of a deer desperately looking for water. Do you see such a longing for God in the church today?
- Have you ever felt down? Do you find it difficult to admit negative emotions like despair? How do you deal with them?
- Try to express your heart to the Lord by composing a prayer. You may use Psalm 42/43 as a pattern.
- How often do you hear the message that Christians are supposed to always be OK?
- How can we preach in such a way that we do not ignore or deny the negative experiences of those we preach to?

Sample sermon outline on Psalm 42/43

Title: Dealing with Negative Emotions: What We Can Learn from Psalm 42/43

1) A person who is close to God is not necessarily always joyful

   a) The psalmist is one who is really close to God
      i) He likens his longing for God to that of a deer desperately longing for water (42:1)
      ii) He addresses God as "my God" (42:1, 5, 11)

   b) Yet he is in tears (42:3)

   c) He is downcast (42:5, 11; 43:5)

2) The importance of being open to God

   a) The psalmist is honest to God about what he really feels towards him
      i) "Why have you forgotten me?" (42:9)
      ii) Compare Psalm 22:1 – "My God, my God, why have you forsaken me?"

   b) The psalmist tells God about what his enemies did to him
      i) Though he feels abandoned by God (42:9), he continues to come to God

c) The psalmist pleads to God for:
   i)   vindication (43:1)
   ii) deliverance (43:1)
   iii) more intimacy with him (43:3–4)

Conclusion: Even our Lord Jesus himself felt downcast (Matt 26:38), and other believers throughout history (see above, Bonhoeffer, Martin Luther).

4

It's OK to Be Sad

"Will you please pray for him?" My pastor-friend asked me this as we stood at the bedside of Eric, a 35-year-old pastor who had suffered a stroke. He had been in a small room in the intensive care unit for a week now. We had to queue to visit him because the hospital allowed only two to three visitors at a time.

I could hardly hear Eric as he struggled to speak, but I could sense his pain. This was not the Eric I knew from seminary days – jolly, talkative, and active. The Eric I saw now could hardly move, was unable to smile, and had tired eyes. I knew we couldn't stay long because he needed to rest, so I prepared to pray. As I closed my eyes, however, I struggled to find the right words to say. I couldn't find any positive words. So I prayed a prayer similar to one of the lament psalms – I expressed sadness, sorrow, and grief to God. Immediately after I prayed, my pastor-friend also prayed. I had thought he'd delegated the praying to me, but realized that maybe he felt there was something missing in my prayer. He then said something in his prayer that made me wonder: "Lord, this sickness does not glorify you. But I pray that Pastor Eric's response to his situation will glorify you."

What is a response that glorifies God when you can hardly speak because of the pain? How do you glorify God when there are lots of uncertainties and questions in your mind? Eric has two children, one of them a newborn baby. I am sure Eric is deeply saddened by what happened to him, and so are his wife and family. Given his situation, his sadness is one that could easily turn to depression.

How do we respond in a way that glorifies God in situations like these?

Only one acceptable response?

We have been taught that in all situations, we should respond positively. I was once listening to a lecture on lament when a framed quotation hanging in a corner of the room caught my attention. It said:

> Happy moments – Praise God
> Difficult moments – Seek God
> Quiet moments – Worship God
> Painful moments – Trust God
> Every moment – Thank God!

The usual response we have for all situations is "Every moment – Thank God!" Come to think of it, we can very easily apply this to Eric's case, can't we? Eric is a pastor. The night before he had that tragic stroke, he had been at the church. The following morning, he could no longer get up and was rushed to the hospital. Should we try to comfort him by singing "It Is Well with My Soul"? Can we encourage him to say, "The Lord giveth and the Lord taketh away"?

I do not want to reject that kind of response. I think it is commendable in some ways. And there are situations when those who have uttered such words have genuinely meant it in their hearts. But it is worrisome when this becomes the only response we know, as if the only response that would glorify God is the positive one.

In the same way, it is not wrong for the church to be a place of celebration. There are many reasons why the church should celebrate. It is when the church is being celebrative all the time, day in and day out, that it becomes a problem. For when the church does not learn how to live with "sadness, brokenness, and questioning," it will not learn how to respond when tragic events occur.[1] What we have to learn is that it is OK to be sad, broken, and lonely when we go through difficult situations.

Different seasons, different responses

Like nature, we go through different seasons of life. In the Philippines we have only two seasons – dry and wet, rainy and sunny. It was only when I lived in England that I appreciated the words of a song that refers to "winter, spring, summer or fall." As the seasons change, so do the surroundings. A field is

---

1. Swinton, *Raging with Compassion*, 92.

green during the wet season and brown and bare during the dry season. It's still the same place, but it looks different. It becomes different. Nature adjusts to its varying seasons.

In the same way, we go through the seasons of our own lives. Old Testament scholar Walter Brueggemann mentions three of these seasons:[2]

1) Season of orientation
2) Season of disorientation
3) Season of new orientation

The season of orientation refers to situations in our life when life is normal. Of course, we know that what is "normal" depends on our circumstances. The heavy traffic in Manila may not seem normal to foreigners visiting for the first time; but for us Filipinos, it's normal. By "normal," I mean it is usual, we can cope with it. Things are not perfect, of course, but life is generally OK. In a season of orientation, our days are like a boat sailing "normally" on the sea. There are some small waves and the wind is blowing, but the sun is shining and the boat is pretty much controllable.

Now imagine that we are sailing along in that boat, and that suddenly we see dark clouds rolling in and obscuring the sun. There is a blast of wind, and the waves are no longer small ripples – they are now huge and violent. Our serenity is shattered. We feel that we may die at any moment. We are not sure if we'll make it – there is no guarantee. And so we cling to our boat for dear life, drenched by the water crashing over us. We are now in an entirely different season, a season of disorientation.

In the season of disorientation, all sense of normal is gone. We look for the ordinary places we know, but they are no longer there. We're lost. We search deep within us for some guidance to ride the raging sea, to no avail. All that's left is our boat, which may be sinking. The death of a loved one, an accident, the loss of a job, or a divorce may lead to a season of disorientation in our lives. What happened to Eric also counts as a season of disorientation.

The good news is that a few months after our visit, Eric was up and about, slowly getting back to his normal routines. He had almost died, but he survived. He was now experiencing what we call the season of new orientation. This is the season "after the storm." Just when we thought our boat would sink, the wind stopped and the waves settled. Think of how Jesus spoke to the wind and the waves when he calmed the storm. What followed

---

2. Walter Brueggemann, *The Message of the Psalms* (Minneapolis, MN: Augsburg, 1984).

was a great stillness – a setting even more peaceful than before the storm. Those who have gone through cancer and recovered know exactly what I am talking about. Just when you thought it was the end of it all, life broke in, bringing new meaning and hope – things you never expected would still be possible. Just when we thought that our suffering would never end, we realize the heavy cloud has been lifted, just like that. Yes, there's a certain feeling of "just like that." Many describe entering this season as living through a very long process of struggle, and then, at the end, feeling that life is returning to them.

Sadly, some people do not reach this season because they decide to end it all by committing suicide. Depressed people sometimes think there is no more end to their darkness, pain and woes. But there is an end to it. It will come. We may not know when, but it will come. And when it does, we just can't wait to celebrate.

A time to dance

Celebration. That's what the believers of old did when they were in a season of new orientation. When their prayers were answered, the Israelites would go to the temple and give a thanksgiving offering, known as the *todah*. An example of a thanksgiving psalm is Psalm 116:

> I love the LORD, for he heard my voice; he heard my cry for mercy. Because he turned his ear to me, I will call on him as long as I live . . . I will sacrifice a thank offering to you and call on the name of the LORD . . . I will fulfill my vows to the LORD in the presence of all his people, in the courts of the house of the LORD – in your midst, Jerusalem. Praise the LORD. (Ps 116:1–2, 17–19)

A worshipper would celebrate with his loved ones. The good thing about the *todah* is that the animal offered would be returned to the one who had brought it, the offerer. He would then cook the meat (people then did not often get the chance to eat meat), and invite his family and friends to partake of the feast. Together, they would celebrate the goodness of the Lord. In the midst of the celebration, the one who had experienced an answer to prayer would stand up and recount what the Lord had done. Psalm 116 gives us some idea of what was usually said in such gatherings.

I've witnessed a modern version of a *todah* in our church. When one of our members survived a kidney transplant, she prepared a feast for the church. There was lots of food; we even had *lechon*, a special roast pig. Together, we rejoiced in what the Lord had done. This member is still alive today, fifteen years after the operation. Isn't that amazing? Occasions like these do call for celebration and thanksgiving. And the Bible, particularly the Psalms, knows well what it means to celebrate. If you read the Psalms you will notice that all the available instruments – cymbals, harp, tambourine, trumpet, etc. – are played when people praise God (see Ps 150). Worshippers also dance as they sing. Remember David dancing with all his might when the Ark of the Covenant was about to enter his house (2 Sam 6:16)? Talk about "praise and worship" as we have come to term it today. The people then had it – and more.

A time to mourn

But they did not always rejoice and dance and sing happy songs. When a season of disorientation struck, like defeat in a war or pests destroying crops, people would go to the temple and, as a community, lament before God.[3] Their type of prayer is known as the communal lament. Psalm 44 is an example of this type of prayer. This psalm begins with a recollection of what God has done in the past; how he defeated his people's enemies, how he saved them and granted them victory.

> We have heard it with our ears, O God; our fathers have told us what you did in their days, in days long ago. With your hand you drove out the nations and planted our fathers; you crushed the peoples and made our fathers flourish. It was not by their sword that they won the land, nor did their arm bring them victory; it was your right hand, your arm, and the light of your face, for you loved them. You are my King and my God, who decrees victories for Jacob. (Ps 44:1–4)

---

3. Hermann Gunkel and Joachim Begrich, *Introduction to the Psalms: The Genres of the Religious Lyric of Israel*, trans. James D. Nogalski (Macon, GA: Mercer University Press, 1998), 13: "Alongside the happy festivals of rejoicing in the community stands the days of lamentation. When crop failure, pestilence, and danger from the enemy afflicted the people, such a day of lamentation was observed. On such occasions all the people would assemble in the sanctuary, tear their clothes, fast, weep, lament, and sound the trumpet."

But in the middle of the psalm, people pour out their hearts to God. They
tell him:

> But now you have rejected and humbled us; you no longer go out
> with our armies. You made us retreat before the enemy, and our
> adversaries have plundered us. You gave us up to be devoured
> like sheep and have scattered us among the nations. (Ps 44:9–11)

We will talk more in detail about this manner of praying, about whether
it's OK to question God or not, in chapter 7. But for now, we can see how
different the response of God's people was when disaster or calamity struck
their community. They did not feel obliged to give thanks or celebrate. No, the
response of the Israelites was not limited to that. God's people knew how to
lament. They even had rituals to accompany their lament. If in thanksgiving
they had the *todah* offering, then during times of lament, they put ashes on
their heads, put on sackcloth, fasted, wept, and even pulled out their hair (see
Ezra 9:3). When an individual was sick or in deep trouble, he or she would
pray a lament psalm. We call this type of psalm an "individual lament psalm,"
and there are a lot of these. There are, in fact, more lament psalms in the book
of Psalms than there are thanksgiving psalms. The problem with our response
today is that we do not even know how to lament, let alone have rituals to
accompany our grieving. As we will see in the next chapter, we do not know
how to mourn.

More than one response

Believers of old responded in a way that matched life's extremes of disorientation
and new orientation, of suffering and celebration. In between, when life
was normal (that is, during seasons of orientation) they also responded
accordingly. They had their own songs and declarations, acknowledging that
life is "normal" because it is God who is at work. The season of orientation
can seem boring to some. For instance, many of us think that when we travel
from one place to another and arrive safely at our destination, that that's just
the way it is. "Why thank God?" some of us would say, "It's just normal." But
for the believers of old, "normal" situations are also opportunities to declare
who God is. One example of a psalm of orientation is Psalm 104:

> Praise the LORD, my soul. LORD my God, you are very great . . .
> He set the earth on its foundations; it can never be moved . . .
> He makes springs pour water into the ravines; it flows between

the mountains. They give water to all the beasts of the field; the wild donkeys quench their thirst. The birds of the air nest by the waters; they sing among the branches . . . He makes grass grow for the cattle, and plants for man to cultivate – bringing forth food from the earth . . . The moon marks off the seasons, and the sun knows when to go down. You bring darkness, it becomes night, and all the beasts of the forest prowl . . . The sun rises, and they steal away; they return and lie down in their dens. Then man goes out to his work, to his labor until evening. How many are your works, LORD! In wisdom you made them all; the earth is full of your creatures.

Thus, we see that as the Israelites went through the different seasons of life, they also had their different sets of responses. New orientation led to celebration and thanksgiving. Disorientation caused them to lament and weep. In both of these, Walter Brueggemann explains, "They have limit expressions for their limit experiences."[4] Limit experiences are those experiences which bring us to the limits, the extremes. The limit could involve positive experiences like healing, resolution, or answered prayer. Or it could involve negative experiences like loss and death. In both situations, we see that God's people had "limit expressions," not just one "limit expression" (singular). They celebrated in new orientation; they lamented in disorientation. And somewhere in the middle, they acknowledged God's presence in the season of orientation.

It's OK to be sad

The main difference with us today is that we have only one response for all the seasons of life. It's the positive response. We do not really know how to express our sadness. We do not have room for our negative experiences in the church. We tend to think that we should wear the same mask for all occasions. We are afraid that if we respond in a negative way, we will be moving away from God. But it is OK for our responses to change as our seasons of life do. For we know there is One who remains constant throughout our changing seasons. He is the one to whom we can go not only in times of thanksgiving and stability but also in times of lament.

---

4. Walter Brueggemann, *The Psalms and the Life of Faith* (Minneapolis, MN: Fortress Press, 1985), 27.

It is important to underline this truth: Our seasons change, as our responses do, but God remains our God. He is our God not only when we are OK, but also when we are not OK. We need not be afraid that our response may not glorify God. In a season of disorientation, it is OK to be sad.

When sadness hits

In times of sadness, David was not ashamed to confess: "For my life is spent with sorrow, and my years with sighing" (Ps 31:10 ESV). In the midst of his sadness David cried out: "How long must I wrestle with my thoughts and every day have sorrow in my heart?" (Ps 13:2). I remember experiencing a similar deep, unceasing sadness when I was away from my home, living in a foreign land.

The psalmist also knows times of loneliness: "I lie awake; I have become like a bird alone on a roof" (Ps 102:7). Think of that image for a moment. Do you sometimes see yourself as being like that bird? Old people can certainly identify with that image. Sociologists tell us that the number of old people will continue to increase because of the rise in life expectancy. Unfortunately, however, "older people have no real place in modern family."[5] My wife Rosemarie used to work with elderly people when we were based in the UK. One day, one of the residents came to her, looked her in the eyes with all the seriousness in the world, and told her: "I only have one piece of advice for you. Three words," she said. "Don't get old." My wife jokingly answered, "It's four words, 'Do not get old.'" But Rosemarie felt the resident's loneliness and fear. "It's really sad," she told me, "when I see them lonely and depressed all day. Some of them don't even want to go out of their room." Rosemarie observed that the depression among the elderly usually peaked during the Christmas season – especially among those no longer visited by their loved ones.

If you are an old person (or a young person who feels old) and you feel this way, there is someone who can identify with your loneliness and sadness. Take to heart the prayer in Psalm 71:9: "Do not cast me away when I am old; do not forsake me when my strength is gone."

---

5. Peter L. Berger and Brigitte Berger, *Sociology: A Biographical Approach* (New York: Penguin Books, 1972), 102–103.

The Son of God was sad

Jesus knew what it means to be filled with joy:

> At that time Jesus, full of joy through the Holy Spirit, said, "I praise you, Father, Lord of heaven and earth, because you have hidden these things from the wise and learned, and revealed them to little children. Yes, Father, for this is what you were pleased to do." (Luke 10:21)

But although Jesus could identify with the season of new orientation, he also had times when he was sad.[6] We can say he knew the sadness that the saddest person in the world experiences. He knew deeply what it means to be sorrowful:

> He took Peter and the two sons of Zebedee along with him, and he began to be sorrowful and troubled. (Matt 26:37)

This was in the Garden of Gethsemane, where Jesus confessed to his disciples, "My soul is overwhelmed with sorrow to the point of death" (v. 38). But Luke tells us that even earlier, as Jesus anticipated his Gethsemane experience and the cross, he was already in distress: "But I have a baptism to undergo, and how distressed I am until it is completed!" (Luke 12:50).

Psychologists tell us that healthy people have a broad range of emotions. They have the ability to feel joyful, sad, angry or mad, down, or afraid. *But they do not get stuck with one emotion.* If you look at Jesus, you will see someone whose emotions are as broad as life itself. He

- shed tears (Luke 19:41)
- was filled with joy (Luke 10:21)
- grieved (Mark 14:34)
- was angry (Mark 3:5)
- got frustrated (Matt 17:17; Mark 8:21)
- was overwhelmed with sadness (Matt 26:37)
- felt sorrow (Luke 7:13)
- showed astonishment and wonder (Mark 6:6; Luke 7:9)

---

6. For a discussion of the emotional life of Jesus, see Peter Scazzero, *The Emotionally Healthy Church: A Strategy for Discipleship that Actually Changes Lives* (Grand Rapids, MI: Zondervan, 2003), 32–33, 75–76; see also, Richard Vincent, "The Emotional Life of Jesus" http://www.theocentric.com/theology/christology/emotional_life_of_jesus.html, accessed March 2011.

- felt distress (Luke 12:50 – distressed over going through Gethsemane and the cross).

Jesus himself went through the three seasons we have looked at, and he responded not just in one way, but in many. How about you?

Three seasons of life

It may be helpful at this point to review the three seasons of life we looked at earlier. There is actually one psalm where all three seasons are present – Psalm 30 (NRSV).[7]

Orientation (6–7a)

As for me, I said in my prosperity,
"I shall never be moved."
By your favor, O LORD,
you had established me as a strong mountain.

Disorientation (7b–10)

You hid your face;
I was dismayed.
To you, O LORD, I cried,
and to the LORD I made supplication:
"What profit is there in my death,
if I go down to the Pit?
Will the dust praise you?
Will it tell of your faithfulness?
Hear, O LORD, and be gracious to me!
O LORD, be my helper!"

---

7. Walter Brueggemann observed the three seasons in Psalm 30 in his book, *The Message of the Psalms*, 24, 50, 122.

New Orientation (11)

You have turned my mourning into dancing;
You have taken off my sackcloth
and clothed me with joy.

Observe the different experiences in each of the three seasons, and the differing responses. In the season of orientation, there is a sense of stability because of the Lord's goodness. This is suddenly shattered by the experience of disorientation in verse 7b. Note that the shift from orientation to disorientation takes place in just a half verse. The psalmist now cries out to the Lord as he feels close to the grave. But then comes the joy that the season of new orientation brings. Looking at these three seasons, pause and ask yourself, "Which season am I in today?" Is it the season of orientation, new orientation, or disorientation?

If you are in a season of disorientation right now, I want to encourage you. If you feel sad, give yourself permission to be sad now. When we are going through suffering some of us tend to rush towards being OK, to deny what we are really feeling or going through. When we go through the different seasons of our life, it is important that we be present where we are so that we will receive whatever gifts our experience may bring us.

I remember talking about the three seasons of life to a group of young business people. One of them asked me, "What should I do when I am in a season of new orientation, because I could experience disorientation again at any time?" Even while in the time of new orientation, this young man couldn't enjoy it; he anticipated a change in seasons and thus could not be present to his own experience. It is the same with people who are in disorientation; they do not want to be in such a season because it is unpleasant, lonely, and sad. But sadness brings its own gift.

Sadness makes our hearts more compassionate and gentle towards others who are suffering. If we have never experienced what it means to be sad and lonely, how will we understand what old people feel? How can we identify with the sadness of children living on the streets, who in the coldness of the night and the heat of the day keep wishing someone would care? How can we enter into the experience of those who have gone through severe marital difficulties? How will we know what it means to be sick for ten years with no one visiting you?

It is when we are present in our disorientation that our experience of new orientation becomes meaningful. Our experience of joy is directly related to our experience of loneliness and sadness. For as the Lebanese writer Kahlil Gibran beautifully puts it:[8]

> Your joy is your sorrow unmasked.
> And the selfsame well from which your laughter
>   rises was oftentimes filled with your tears.
> And how else can it be?
> The deeper that sorrow carves into your being,
>   the more joy you can contain.
> Is not the cup that holds your wine the very
>   cup that was burned in the potter's oven?
> And is not the lute that soothes your spirit,
>   the very wood that was hollowed with knives?
> When you are joyous, look deep into your heart
>   and you shall find it is only that which
>   has given you sorrow that is giving you joy.
> When you are sorrowful look again in your heart,
>   and you shall see that in truth you are weeping
>   for that which has been your delight.
> Some of you say, "Joy is greater than sorrow,"
>   and others say, "Nay, sorrow is the greater."
> But I say unto you, they are inseparable.
> Together they come, and when one sits alone
>   with you at your board, remember that
>   the other is asleep upon your bed.
> Verily you are suspended like scales between
>   your sorrow and your joy.
> Only when you are empty are you
>   at standstill and balanced.
> When the treasure-keeper lifts you to weigh
>   his gold and his silver, needs must your joy
>   or your sorrow rise or fall.

---

8. Kahlil Gibran, *The Prophet* (London: Heinemann, 1926), 36–37.

Encountering a psalm

Read Psalm 30.

- In this chapter we have learned about the three seasons of life: orientation, disorientation, and new orientation. In which season are you today? What is it about your own situation that leads you to say you are in this particular season?

- Is it true that Christians today tend to have only one response to all situations – the positive response?

- Does your church/community allow the expression of grief and sorrow? Do you have opportunities to lament as a congregation and not just during prayer meetings or small groups? Do you think it is necessary for the church to learn how to lament?

- How do you move from disorientation to new orientation? How can the lament psalms help us in this shift?

- Reflect on the sermons you have preached on for the past six months. How many of them relate to the season of disorientation?

- What can we learn from the discussion of the different seasons of life when it comes to how we plan our sermons?

- Can you identify two psalms for each of the three seasons of life (e.g. orientation – Psalm 103; disorientation – Psalm 22; new orientation – Psalm 116)?

5

It's OK to Cry

I once attended the funeral service of the former president of one of the biggest denominations in the Philippines. The very title of the service was revealing: "Celebrating the Life of the Reverend Juan Garcia" (not his real name). The title hinted that we were there not to mourn but to thank the Lord for the life of this man of God. In fact the very absence of mourning or crying was conspicuous. I was seated in the second row of the church and, as I looked around me, there was not one person crying. The sermon was the usual funeral message that focused on the confidence we have in the Lord – the assurance that our brother is now with the Lord and that at the end, God will resurrect him. So why mourn? Even the final words of the president's wife were all positive. She was praising and thanking God.

Mourning: Then and now

Actually, we Filipinos are not like this. It is common practice among Filipinos to mourn the dead. There is usually a lot of crying and wailing in funerals. I remember when my grandfather, who was a former mayor of our town in Pangasinan, died. I was only about six years old then. On the day he died, he had been visiting us in our house in Dagupan. That morning, he had come for a visit, as he was in town for a check-up. I left him because I needed to go to school. When I returned home later that day, *Lolo* was already in the morgue. I was in shock. This was my first experience of someone close to me dying.

The day of the interment we walked from the house of my *lolo* to the cemetery – a long walk. During that procession we were crying, wailing even. I was walking behind the car carrying his body and as I held on to the back of the vehicle, I was also crying. The music being played also added to the somber mood. At the cemetery, the scene became even more intense. As *Lolo*'s casket was lowered into the ground, some people collapsed in grief.

Today, this practice of mourning is lost and is even considered inappropriate in some Christian traditions.[1] This is especially true if the one who died is a believer, more so if he is a pastor or a prominent leader. We feel that we don't need to mourn. We reason that he is now with the Lord and so is in a more blessed state. So why mourn? I have even seen a pastor rebuking a church member during a funeral because she was weeping over the death of her husband! Another member of that church, in fact, told me they no longer use the word "condolences."

When we are with loved ones who are still unbelievers, we want to show them we are OK *because we are Christians*. These days, it is common to see funeral services being used by Christians as opportunities for evangelism and witnessing. The focus is not on mourning – if there is mourning at all. I once officiated a funeral service where the sister of the person who had died just could not contain herself when the casket was about to be lowered into the grave. She started wailing and weeping. A week after the funeral service this believer told me, "I'm so glad they did not record the audio of the funeral, so that no one will hear how I cried there."

Jesus wept

Why are we ashamed to cry? Why are we ashamed to cry when our Master himself did not care if people saw or heard him weep over the death of his friend Lazarus? "Jesus wept," the Bible tells us. There is something in these two words – this verse – that calls our attention. John 11:35 is the shortest verse in the Bible. Maybe the one who put the verse numbers of the Bible knew he had to pause when he read those two words. Maybe he felt something. That may have been the reason why he isolated those words "Jesus wept." It could be that he was so moved by the story that he dropped what he was doing and wept too. This is like the famous news photographer Adrees Latif's reaction when he saw how the Asian tsunami in 2011 had wiped out an entire town in Japan: "I have seen similar disasters – I covered the (2004 Indian Ocean) tsunami in Thailand – but I have never seen anything like this in my life,"

---

1. There has been a decline in the practice of mourning for the dead over the last century in many societies around the world, not just among Christians. See James Wilce, *Crying Shame: Metaculture, Modernity, and the Exaggerated Death of Lament* (Oxford: Wiley-Blackwell, 2009).

Latif said. "I stopped shooting for a while to look out at the town, and I just stood there in disbelief."[2]

Even in the Old Testament, God is presented as one who is in pain (see Hos 11:8 and Num 14:11). The Japanese theologian Kazoh Kitamori speaks about the "pain of God" in the Old Testament. "The heart of the gospel," writes Kitamori, "was revealed to me as the pain of God."[3] I think that's the reason why the prophet Jeremiah was not afraid to shed tears. It was because he knew the pain of God. Only those who know how to cry can understand the heart of God.

If this is the case, then why is there an absence of mourning in our churches today?

Why we don't cry

I think a major part of the reason comes from how we understand certain passages in the New Testament. These passages, taken on their own as sweeping statements, can mean there is no more need for mourning. Foremost among these are passages teaching that God is in control and that he is good all the time. If God is in control and is good, then why mourn when you experience calamity, an accident, or even the loss of a loved one? We have read that our sufferings make us stronger (Jas 1:2–4), and that God works in all things for our good (Rom 8:28). As one devotional author explains, "Whatever your circumstances, and however difficult they may be, the truth is that they are ordained by God for you as part of his overall plan for your life. God does nothing, or allows nothing, without a purpose. And his purposes, however mysterious and inscrutable they may be to us, are always for his glory and our ultimate good."[4] Thus, instead of mourning, Christians supposedly should thank the Lord (1 Thess 5:18).

Second is the teaching to "rejoice in the Lord always" (Phil 4:4). So why do we have to mourn? Someone even said that if we do not rejoice, we are

---

2. "My Paper," a newspaper, a Singapore Holdings Publication, 15 March 2011, p. A11.

3. Kazoh Kitamori, *Theology of the Pain of God* (Richmond, VA: John Knox Press, 1965), 19. The pain of God results from God's desire to love the unworthy yet at the same time, punish the guilty. This brings about the struggle within God; it brings him pain. One passage in Hosea 11:8 tells us: "How can I give you up, O Ephraim? How can I hand you over, O Israel? How can I make you like Admah? How can I treat you like Zeboiim? My heart recoils within me; my compassion grows warm and tender" (ESV).

4. Jerry Bridges, *Respectable Sins: Confronting the Sins We Tolerate* (Colorado Springs, CO: NavPress, 2007), 74.

actually sinning: "Joy is a command. Joylessness is a serious sin."[5] Moreover, we also find passages that tell us that those who suffer because of persecution should rejoice. Didn't Jesus tell us to do so? "Blessed are you when people insult you, persecute you and falsely say all kinds of evil against you because of me. Rejoice and be glad, because great is your reward in heaven, for in the same way they persecuted the prophets who were before you" (Matt 5:11–12). That is what Paul and Silas were doing in Acts 16:25: "About midnight Paul and Silas were praying and singing hymns to God, and the other prisoners were listening to them." While they were in prison, they were singing songs.

But I have some questions:

- Does the truth that God is in control and that he works in everything for the good of those who are called by him and love him mean we will no longer have to mourn?
- Is it a sign of weak faith to mourn the loss of our loved ones?
- Does the command to "rejoice in the Lord always" mean there must be no more mourning?
- When people are persecuted because of their faith, is it wrong for them to cry and weep?
- Is it a sign of weak faith when Christians mourn for their loved ones who have been martyred?

I will try to answer these questions. But let me be clear – I agree that joy occupies a central place in the life of faith; it is an important quality of a growing Christian. It is the fruit of the Holy Spirit (Gal 5:22–23). As we have seen earlier, the traditional Christian teaching on rejoicing and trusting in God in any situation is based in the Scriptures. Jesus came that we might have life and have it to the full (John 10:10), and it is his desire that our joy be complete (John 15:11). Paul's instruction to rejoice in the Lord affirms this (Phil 4:4).

But we also see in the New Testament that the same Apostle Paul who commands us to rejoice in the Lord also encourages us to "mourn with those who mourn," even as he instructs us to "rejoice with those who rejoice" (Rom 12:15). He exhorts us to "carry each other's burdens" (Gal 6:2) and to "encourage one another" (1 Thess 5:11). This means that even though Paul commands Christians to rejoice always, he understands that there will be times when they will have to mourn. If we are encouraged to mourn with

5. John Ortberg, *Life to the Max: Daring to Love, Laugh and Loosen Up* (Manila: OMF Literature, Inc., 2007 [orig. Zondervan as *Living the God Life*, 2004]), 83.

those who mourn, how much more for our own losses, like the death of our own loved one? Even Jesus wept when his friend Lazarus died (John 11).

I think the problem begins when we take one command given in a particular context and apply it to all situations of our life. This happens when a word given in a season of orientation or new orientation is applied even to times of disorientation (see ch. 2). We actually find an equivalent of Philippians 4:4 ("rejoice in the Lord always") in the Psalms. David declares in Psalm 34:1: "I will bless the LORD *at all times*." But in the very next psalm (Ps 35), David is already weeping: "Yet when they were ill, I put on sackcloth and humbled myself with fasting. When my prayers returned to me unanswered, I went about *mourning* as though for my friend or brother. I bowed my head in grief as though *weeping* for my mother" (Ps 35:13–14, emphasis mine).

I think another problem is we go to the extreme of thinking that rejoicing is not possible if there is mourning. But remember, although Jesus said, "Rejoice when people persecute you," he did not say, "Do not weep or cry when people persecute you." In fact, as we will see later, Jesus tells his own disciples that they will weep. And by the way, when Jesus talks about the fullness of life (e.g. John 10:10), we may interpret this to mean a life that manifests a broad range of human emotions. The emotional life of Jesus is an example of this (see ch. 2).

It's OK to mourn the loss of a loved one

It is OK to mourn the loss of a loved one. When we weep or mourn for our loved one, this does not mean that our faith is weak. If our departed loved one is a believer, our mourning does not mean that we doubt the destiny of his or her soul. We mourn because we miss our dear brother or sister. We mourn because we know we will not see our loved one again for some time. Psychologist Bruce Narramore said it was only because of his years as a counselor that he understood the meaning of "Blessed are those who mourn." He realized that the reason why he mourns with those who mourn is because he loves them. The other side of sadness is love.[6]

Many who have lost a spouse say they feel paralyzed. This experience is part of mourning, and people who say this are just being honest about what they truly feel. It is natural, and allowing yourself to be natural may be what is

---

6. Bruce Narramore, "Helping People Grow from the Inside Out," a lecture presented in Manila, 2011.

needed at the moment. I like what one priest said when our former president Cory Aquino died: "Lord, we believe Cory is already with you and that she is now happy. But to be honest about it, we feel sad, we feel orphaned." In the play *King Lear*, the Duke of Albany witnesses the king's weeping over his dead daughter and says:

> "The weight of this sad time we must obey;
> Speak what we feel, not what we ought to say."[7]

At the beginning of this chapter, I mentioned the funeral service of the president of a denomination and his wife's positive words. But while she was expressing her thanksgiving and praise to God for the life of her husband, I saw her tears. They flowed like a river as she spoke. Somehow, the suffering and pain she experienced found their way out through her tears. I am glad she wept.

Mourning is part of the process of restoration

Grieving is the single most important thing we do to experience the healing of broken emotions. Without properly grieving or mourning our suffering, there will be no restoration. That is why we find a lot of crying and weeping in the Bible. Even the macho man David cried too, and quite a lot at that!

- Psalm 3:4 – "To the LORD I cry aloud, and he answers me from his holy hill."

  We usually hear women crying aloud or wailing. But for a man to cry aloud – that is really something. Here we find David doing just that. In his next prayers, we hear him crying again.

- Psalm 5:2 – "Listen to my cry for help, my King and my God, for to you I pray."

- Psalm 17:1 – "Hear, O LORD, my righteous plea; listen to my cry."

- Psalm 22:2 – "O my God, I cry out by day, but you do not answer, by night, and am not silent."

"Men don't cry," we often hear. Maybe that's one reason why more men than women die of heart attacks. Even after the death of a loved one, a man, especially if he is the eldest in the family, will not cry. He will do everything to maintain his "composure." He feels that he should give courage to the rest of the family. So he holds his tears within himself.

---

7. *King Lear*, act 5, sc. 3, lines 305–307; quoted in Samuel E. Balentine, *Prayer in the Hebrew Bible* (Minneapolis, MN: Fortress Press, 1993), 146.

David does not hold his tears; he lets them flow. But more than that, he cries to the Lord. That is very important. A lot of people today are crying, but they feel they are crying alone, with no one to listen to their cries. David cries, he weeps; but he knows he is not alone. He knows the Lord is listening to him. And so to the Lord he turns: "I cry out to God Most High" (Ps 57:2).

And as David pours out his heart to the Lord, something happens within him, enabling him to look into his trouble. He gathers enough courage to confront his situation. His vision becomes clearer as his eyes are washed with tears.

Someone once asked my church's former senior pastor, "Why is your face always radiant?" He answered, "*Dahil ibinabad sa luha*" [Because it has been immersed in tears]. In Psalm 57:4 David was able to capture what he felt about his situation:

> I am in the midst of lions;
> I lie among ravenous beasts –
> men whose teeth are spears and arrows,
> whose tongues are sharp swords.

David was able to name his situation. Psychologists tell us that the ability to name our struggle is an important step towards our restoration. The use of imagery involving lions and ravenous beasts helped David express what he felt about his circumstances. It helped him establish some control over his situation because now he had a "name" for it.

All of us have had past experiences that we do not want to remember any more. Maybe because they are too painful. But a helpful exercise is to give a name or description for our pain. The following poem is an example of how one person was able to get over his painful experience by describing it and, in the process, accepting it:[8]

> I could not have known by then
> That I would learn to love this memory
> Run it smooth between my fingers,
> A velvety stone found on a beautiful beach.
> I hold this stone like a charm.
> The charm is not the pain.
> But when I give myself back my pain,

---

8. The poem is by Joe Kogel, cited in James D. Whitehead and Evelyn Eaton Whitehead, *Shadows of the Heart: A Spirituality of the Negative Emotions* (New York: Crossroads, 1994), 18.

> I make myself real
> And when I am real, I'm lucky.
> I am lucky knowing it was wrong and a lie.
> What we called a happy family was not.
> I . . . hid in small rooms. Until now.

Psychologist James Whitehead explains: "Healing begins 'when I give myself back my pain.' Naming the pain – 'what we called a happy family was not' – rescues his past from oblivion. The pretense of a happy family and the distortions demanded to protect this illusion fall away. 'I make myself real.'"[9]

Whitehead continues: "Mourning is the *work* of grief. If we refuse the work of mourning, our grief will consume us. But when we mourn, we begin to transform pain into suffering – a sorrow that will enrich instead of cripple."[10]

It was when David poured out his heart and confronted his situation by naming it that he experienced restoration. In the midst of all his troubles he was able to shout:

> Be exalted, O God, above the heavens;
>   let your glory be over all the earth. (Ps 57:5, 11)

Mourning marks the road to glory

David's experience – that of flowing from tears to exaltation – is a miniature depiction of the overall movement of the life of faith. We will also experience joy and exaltation. In the meantime, however, we can draw strength from what Jesus told his disciples:

> "I tell you the truth, you will weep and mourn while the world rejoices. You will grieve, but your grief will turn to joy. A woman giving birth to a child has pain because her time has come; but when her baby is born she forgets the anguish because of her joy that a child is born into the world. So with you: Now is your time of grief, but I will see you again and you will rejoice, and no one will take away your joy." (John 16:20–22)

---

9. Ibid., 19.
10. Ibid., 26.

Mothers can readily identify with the words of Jesus here. They know how painful the process of giving birth is. But it is the experience of holding their baby after the painful process of delivery that makes them forget their pain. This illustrates our present and future experiences. We will rejoice in the future, but in the present we will "weep and mourn while the world rejoices."

In a world that constantly rejects God's rule and his kingdom, God's people will inevitably mourn. In a society that continues to reject its Creator, we will mourn. And this is OK. Jesus actually calls those who mourn, "blessed." "Blessed are those who mourn, for they will be comforted" (Matt 5:4). Note: It is those who mourn who will be comforted.

But mourning for what? Matthew 5:4 does not say what things the people here are mourning about, or what the cause of their mourning is. We can infer that mourning here comes as a result of the believers' desire to live righteously in the midst of a corrupt and evil world. In their desire to do what is right, Christians will struggle. They will mourn. They will be like "resident aliens,"[11] always going against the tide. That is the experience of the psalmist: "My eyes shed streams of tears, because people do not keep your law" (Ps 119:136 ESV). The Apostle Paul too is full of tears as he recalls how many live as enemies of the gospel: "For, as I have often told you before and now say again even with tears, many live as enemies of the cross of Christ" (Phil 3:18). Talk about the weeping Paul. Yes, it is the same man who commands us to "rejoice in the Lord always." But here we find him in tears too.

How about Christians who are persecuted and the loved ones of those who have been martyred? Is it all right for them to mourn? I think so. The reality is that even though Jesus tells us to rejoice when we are persecuted, we also find occasions in the Bible and in our present day when persecuted Christians cried and mourned. One Indonesian Christian leader told me that when a young believer saw how her friend had been beaten up and persecuted, she suffered shock; she no longer went to church. I think her pain was too much and that there was no room in the church for mourning, so she left. Those who have studied occasions of persecution in modern times tell us that even the most mature believer can be traumatized in the face of persecution.[12] When we turn to the Bible, we also find the mourning of those

---

11. I borrow the phrase, "resident aliens" from William Willimon and Stanley Hauerwas, *Resident Aliens* (Nashville, TN: Abingdon Press, 1989).

12. See the Bad Urach Statement, a consultation on "Developing an evangelical theology of suffering, persecution and martyrdom for the global church in mission," conducted in Germany, September 2009.

who are persecuted or facing martyrdom. The book of Revelation gives us a glimpse of the experience of people who have been martyred. They are crying out to God:

> When he opened the fifth seal, I saw under the altar the souls of those who had been slain for the word of God and for the witness they had borne. They cried out with a loud voice, "O Sovereign Lord, holy and true, how long before you will judge and avenge our blood on those who dwell on the earth?" (Rev 6:9–10 ESV)

The cry, "how long?" in Revelation 6 also recalls the similar cry in the lament psalms, like the one in Psalm 13:1–2:

> How long, LORD? Will you forget me forever? How long will you hide your face from me? How long must I wrestle with my thoughts and day after day have sorrow in my heart? How long will my enemy triumph over me?

The passage in Revelation tells us that persecuted believers mourn too. The martyrs in the book of Revelation are crying out to God for justice and vindication. And it is OK. They know they have suffered for Christ; they have lost their lives for him. And yet, here they are crying out to God in a cry of lament.

Serving the Lord and doing his will is certainly not easy; it involves great sacrifice. And there will be times when we will mourn. We will cry. The Apostle Paul tells us how he served the Lord with tears: "I served the Lord with great humility and with tears . . . for three years I never stopped warning each of you night and day with tears" (Acts 20:19, 31; cf. 2 Cor 2:4). The tears here do not explicitly mean that Paul was mourning. But as an apostle and a missionary pastor, Paul is telling us that he himself has gone through a lot of suffering. As he writes to the church in Corinth, "We do not want you to be uninformed, brothers, about the hardships we suffered in the province of Asia. We were under great pressure, far beyond our ability to endure, so that we despaired even of life" (2 Cor 1:8). He "despaired even of life." In addition to all these, Paul tells us how his concern for the churches often brought him anxiety (2 Cor 11:28).

Thus, in various ways and often as a result of our striving to serve the Lord in a broken world, we will mourn. We will weep for the loss of our loved ones. We will grieve for the injustice and evil in our world. We will cry out because of our experiences of persecution. And it is OK.

The overall movement of the life of faith is towards joy and peace, rejoicing and celebration. Our lives should be marked with joy. But there are times when we find ourselves at the opposite end – weeping, agonizing, crying, mourning, groaning. Yet the amazing thing is that our God is with us even in the dark and lonely places. In the same way that the Spirit helps us in our weaknesses when we do not know how to pray, the Spirit also stays with us in our struggles to find our way towards joy and peace. "The Spirit helps us in our weakness. We do not know what we ought to pray for, but the Spirit himself intercedes for us with groans that words cannot express" (Rom 8:26). It is remarkable that Romans 8:26 tells us that the Spirit "intercedes for us with *groans*." God is with us in our brokenness. And the book of Revelation tells us that one day, when the new heaven and the new earth come, "He will wipe away every tear from their eyes" (Rev 21:4 ESV). The fact that God will wipe away our tears indicates that before that great day, God's people will cry . . . they will mourn. They will mourn even though they know God is in control. If you do not have any tears in your eyes, what will Jesus wipe away when he comes?

We will still mourn

We live in a broken world. Like the rest of humanity, Christians are vulnerable to sickness, violence, calamity, and the evil in society. When Typhoon Ondoy flooded Manila, or when Typhoon Yolanda (Haiyan) devastated Tacloban, it was not just the unbelievers who were affected. Even believers lost not only their properties but the lives of their loved ones. There is no such thing as immunity from pain. The truth that God is in control does not mean we will no longer mourn over our sufferings arising from living in a broken world. The truth of God being in control and working together in all things for our good (Rom 8:28) does not negate the experience of mourning or crying. It does not mean that everything will be smooth and easy. God often accomplishes his plans through difficult and challenging situations, as we can see in the story of Joseph.

The story of Joseph

The story of Joseph in the book of Genesis is a classic illustration of the truth in Romans 8:28. God revealed his plan for Joseph in a dream. He dreamed one night that the sheaves of his brothers were all bowing down before his sheaf. Whatever the meaning of this dream may have been, we now know that God had a great plan for this young man.

We know what happened after – everything that happened was actually contrary to Joseph's dreams! His brothers would have killed him, had it not been for his brother Reuben who protected him. What his brothers did to Joseph was actually worse than killing him. They sold him as a slave and later told their father that he was already dead, having been killed by some ferocious animal. Joseph later found himself a slave in Egypt. Here, he is in one of the most difficult situations in his life – he is a foreigner with no name, no rights, no future, no worth. Yet we are told in Genesis 39 – precisely at the lowest point in his life – that "the LORD was with Joseph." This phrase occurs four times in the chapter – twice when he was sold as a slave to Potiphar (vv. 2–3), and twice when he was unjustly imprisoned for an act he did not commit (vv. 21, 23). This was when Mrs Potiphar accused him of attempting to rape her, when in fact it was she who had wanted to take advantage of the young Israelite slave.

Here is a clear example of the truth in Romans 8:28. God worked out his plan even through the difficult experiences and suffering of Joseph. Years later, Joseph would tell his brothers: "You intended to harm me, but God intended it for good to accomplish what is now being done, the saving of many lives" (Gen 50:20). Thus, like the ending in a fairy tale, we find Joseph rising from the depths of the pit to the right hand of Pharaoh. Pharaoh actually gives Joseph charge over the whole of Egypt.

When I read the story of Joseph, especially Genesis 37 and 39, one of the questions I asked was, "Didn't Joseph feel lonely, angry, or depressed?" There is nothing in these chapters about his reaction. But a closer reading of the chapters that follow reveals the deeper reality of the pain and hurt Joseph experienced through all those years in Egypt. This we begin to see when he was in prison, where two of Pharaoh's officials had also been sent. The two officials had each had dreams that Joseph was able to interpret. Knowing that the chief cupbearer would be restored to his position, Joseph requested, "Only remember me, when it is well with you, and please do me the kindness to mention me to Pharaoh, and so get me out of this house" (Gen 40:14 ESV). Joseph also confided to the cupbearer his experience, "For I was indeed stolen out of the land of the Hebrews, and here also I have done nothing that they should put me into the pit" (v. 15 ESV). This was not what had happened to Joseph. He had not been "stolen." But I think his version of the story highlights the sense of violence Joseph felt as a result of what his brothers had done to him.

The chief cupbearer, unfortunately, forgot about Joseph. And for two years Joseph waited desperately. No doubt he also cried – the man whom he had hoped would help him get out of that dark prison had forgotten about him. It had to take two more years and another dream, this time of Pharaoh himself, for the cupbearer to realize his serious lapse.

Later, in Genesis 41, we get another glimpse of the deep pain Joseph must have felt throughout those early years in Egypt. The names he gave his two sons – Manasseh and Ephraim – are names that reflect Joseph's feelings of all that had happened to him. "Joseph called the name of the firstborn Manasseh, 'For,' he said, 'God has made me forget *all my hardship* and all my father's house.' The name of the second he called Ephraim, 'For God has made me fruitful in the land of *my affliction.*'" (Gen 41:51–52 ESV, emphasis mine). Notice the names he gave his two children; they are names that describe his experience – "all my hardship" and "affliction."

And then when Joseph finally met his brothers again, he was all tears. I tried counting how many times he wept. He wept seven times – in Genesis 42:24; 43:30; 45:2; 45:14; 46:29; 50:1, and 50:17. Indeed, we can say that he seems the most emotional of the patriarchs. Tears are very powerful expressions of what's within our hearts. The psalmist says, "My tears have been my food day and night" (Ps 42:3). The tears of Joseph can mean a myriad of things – they could have been tears of joy upon seeing his family. But they could have also been tears of pain and agony for the rejection and abandonment he had suffered from those closest to him, and for all the injustices he had experienced. Joseph wept when he first saw his brothers, especially his own brother Benjamin; when he revealed himself to them, reminding them of what they had actually done to him – "I am your brother Joseph, whom you sold." For all the neatness and clarity of the fulfillment of God's plan for Joseph, not everything was tidy after all. Indeed, the story of Joseph tells us that the fulfillment of God's plan in our lives does not mean that everything will be all right. There will be times when it will really hurt, when we will, in fact, mourn.

I remember one period when I mourned. It was during the last year of my PhD in the UK. Three years before, I had gone to the UK with my family to begin my studies. I had been excited then, fresh and eager to start right away. And that's what I did. During the first month of my studies, I already wrote my first paper. I worked hard during those three years, and was actually done at the end of that period. But I remember that day when my examiners told me I had passed. Finally, I had finished the task. But I also felt I was "finished." All the exhaustion, labor, effort, and all the adjustments that we had gone through as a family had taken their toll on me. Coming out of the examination room that memorable day, I didn't want to see anybody. I didn't want anyone to see me. I actually slipped out of the school without anyone noticing me. I didn't know what to do or where to go. The PhD program had been my life for the past three years, and now it was done. I was done. And in the few months after, I struggled to pick up the pieces. Some mornings I would wake up and wish that the sun had never risen. I felt like a "man without strength" (Ps 88:4).

One Sunday, I attended the vesper service of an Anglican church. "You are the everlasting God" were some of the words in the song the congregation was singing that night. We all stood and sang, "You are the everlasting God, you never grow weak or weary." I couldn't contain myself. I couldn't continue singing. Before I realized it, I was already crying – no, I was weeping. And I was telling the Lord, "Lord, you never grow weary, but me, I am so tired." I just sat down and wept. That's all I remember about the whole service. As I wept, I realized and felt God telling me, "It's OK . . . it's OK to cry."

There are times when God wants you to just cry. When was the last time you cried?

Some people stop themselves from crying because it can make them feel vulnerable to whatever it is they are afraid of. What they do not realize, however, is that it's OK to be afraid, as we'll see in the next chapter.

Encountering a psalm

Read Psalm 57.

- David cried a lot in the Psalms, as we saw in this chapter. When was the last time you cried?
- Do you think it's OK for Christians to mourn when they experience loss?
- How can we create spaces for mourning in our churches or communities? Can you think of creative activities to help us incorporate the practice of mourning in our churches?
- In Psalm 57:4 and 6, David describes or "names" his own experience. Below are some images and descriptions of suffering in the Psalms. Which one best describes your situation? Or if none of them fit your situation, how would you describe it? Write your personal description on the blank lines at the end.
  - "My soul is in the midst of lions; I lie down amid fiery beasts" (Ps 57:4 ESV).
  - "They set a net for my steps; my soul was bowed down. They dug a pit in my way" (Ps 57:6 ESV).
  - "Oh, that I had wings like a dove! I would fly away and be at rest" (Ps 55:6 ESV).
  - "I am a worm and not a man, scorned by mankind and despised by the people" (Ps 22:6 ESV).
  - "I am poured out like water, and all my bones are out of joint; my heart is like wax; it is melted within my breast" (Ps 22:14 ESV).
  - "I am weary with my moaning; every night I flood my bed with tears; I drench my couch with my weeping" (Ps 6:6 ESV).
  - "I am like a lonely sparrow on the housetop" (Ps 102:7 ESV).
  - _____

- Using the image or description you have chosen or written down, come to the Lord in prayer and express your heart to him. You may write down your own prayer.
- The NT urges us to "rejoice in the Lord always" (Phil 4:4). And yet the reality of life, as confirmed by the Scriptures themselves (e.g. Rom 12:15), tells us that there are also times when we will weep. How can you preach in such a way that you do not one-

sidedly promote rejoicing? How do you make room for mourning in your preaching?

- How do you avoid an overemphasis on the negative (weeping)? When do you know it is time to move on?

For a sample sermon outline of Psalm 57, see the Appendix.

6

It's OK to Be Afraid

It was dark. The lights had been turned off for the film showing. Our church was so full of people that you could hardly walk through. Among those who had come was a couple from the neighborhood – the husband was a police captain. The film showing was a major project of our youth group and I, the inexperienced 20-year-old youth pastor, was standing on the street outside the church, trying to make sure that everything was all right. It was my first time to lead and coordinate such an event.

Suddenly, I heard a violent commotion inside the church. Before I could even run in, our policeman-guest was dragging one of my youth leaders out into the street. The captain was shouting and burning in anger, and he was about to punch my youth leader, when I intervened. "Why, what's the matter?" I asked. "This guy!" he shouted, gripping the young man's collar. "He took advantage of my wife! He touched her legs!" Trembling, I said to him, "I'm so sorry for what happened. I'll try to talk with him. But please don't hurt him." He let go of my friend, but by this time everyone inside the church had come out into the street. The live action had caught their attention and concern, and they forgot about the film.

I don't remember how I got home that night or what I did next. Maybe I did not do anything, because I was so afraid. I had been in charge of the event, so I felt responsible for what had happened. I felt like a failure. Fearful thoughts rammed against my mind: *What will our church leaders say? What if the captain returns? What if he tries to hurt my youth leader?* I didn't know what to do; I didn't know how to fix the problem. I remember sitting inside the house, anxious, my heart pounding, so afraid to even hear a sound or voice from outside.

That was one instance in my life when I was really afraid. Can you also remember a time when you were afraid? Your experience may not have been as intense as mine, or perhaps it may have been far more horrifying. All of us have experienced being afraid. Of course, fear, like any emotion, can turn into a destructive force. Sadness can turn to depression, anger can turn to bitterness, and fear can paralyze us. There is no question about it; all of us have our own fears.

Some people are afraid of the dark. I myself struggled with this fear for a long time because of the stories my grandmother told us while we were growing up. Outside the gate of my *lola's* house was a stone bench. We would all go out when there was a full moon and we would sit around her, and listen as she told us about the things she heard or saw – about ghosts. I would be afraid to go to the kitchen by myself after that.

We all have our fears. I know of a pastor who is afraid to ride an airplane; so he travels by land or by boat even though this takes much longer. *At least, he thinks, there are more chances of surviving in case of an emergency.* There are men who are afraid of their wives and vice-versa. Some drivers in our country are afraid of traffic police. They have to follow the rules when they see a police or MMDA officer around because they fear getting caught. Many people, on the other hand, are afraid of getting old. As I mentioned earlier, my wife used to work among the elderly. One of them gave her this advice, "Don't get old."

Psychologists tell us two common fears are the fear of rejection and the fear of failure. The two are actually related. Some people hide their true selves because they are afraid that if others get to know who they really are, they will be rejected. This would be the ultimate failure. Many avoid taking risks because success cannot be guaranteed – they are afraid of the hopelessness and disappointment that failure may bring.

We all have our fears. But as Christians, is it all right for us to be afraid? Is it a sign of weak faith when we are afraid? Should we admit being afraid?

Should Christians be unafraid?

"You should not be afraid" I heard one Christian leader tell a group of his fellow church members. This is a common reminder among our churches – for didn't the Bible command us not to be afraid? In fact, the words "Do not be afraid" occur many times in the Bible – they are mentioned around one hundred times. So why be afraid? Won't we be violating this command if we allow ourselves to be afraid?

I don't think so. When we turn to our Bible, we realize that many of God's people – including some of the best-known leaders in the Bible – experienced feeling afraid.

Moses is one such example. Wishing to make a difference, the young Moses one day tried to save an Israelite, and ended up murdering an Egyptian. The problem was that others came to know about his crime. And when Moses realized this, he became so afraid that he ran for his life – and never went back to Egypt for forty long years. It was at the end of those years when God called Moses. In a desert far away, on what is known as the mountain of God, the Lord called to him from a burning bush. "Moses, Moses," God said. Naturally, Moses was afraid. God told him not to come near, for the place he was standing on was holy ground. God then introduced himself as "the God of Abraham, the God of Isaac, and the God of Jacob." He told Moses that he had seen and felt what the Israelites were going through, and that he was concerned about them (Exod 3:6–9).

Moses was all ears and didn't say a word during God's rather long introductory speech . . . until God said, "So now, go. I am sending you to Pharaoh to bring my people the Israelites out of Egypt" (Exod 3:10). When Moses heard these words, he suddenly spoke up, like a student in class raising his hand to call the attention of the teacher. "Who am I?" he said to God, "I don't know how to speak." This was his first excuse in a series of excuses. God answered all his excuses one by one. And finally, running out of excuses, Moses told God, "Send someone else."

We may ask, "Why did Moses respond as he did?" Was he still afraid of the people who knew about his crime? After forty years? Or was he more afraid that he would be a failure as a leader? Exodus 3 and 4 show us that Moses was hesitant to obey God because he was afraid. When he heard that God was sending him back to Egypt, all his old fears were suddenly unleashed, like a rushing river engulfing him.

Well, God has his own way. Moses eventually became the leader of the Israelites. In fact, he became one of Israel's greatest and most revered leaders. But even as a leader, he still experienced being afraid. Remember that time when the Egyptians were pursuing the Israelites? God's people found themselves trapped because they were surrounded by mountains with the Red Sea lying before them. I tell you, the Israelites were afraid to the max; they started crying and blaming Moses (Exod 14:10–12). What did Moses tell them? Like a strong leader, Moses stood up and said to the people:

> Fear not, stand firm, and see the salvation of the LORD, which he
> will work for you today. For the Egyptians whom you see today,
> you shall never see again. The LORD will fight for you, and you
> have only to be silent. (Exod 14:13–14 ESV)

It would appear from what Moses was saying here that he was very much in control, with no fear at all. Yet the very next verse tells us that Moses was crying. God had to tell him to stop crying, to move on and to lead the people – "Why do you cry to me? Tell the people of Israel to go forward" (v. 15 ESV). That's how leaders usually behave. In front of their members, they appear strong, but inside, they are crying. They are afraid.

It's not just Moses who was afraid. The prophet Jeremiah also knew how it was to be afraid. And why wouldn't he be? God called him during a time when people listened only to leaders who were elderly and had white hair. Jeremiah was still very young. And so God had to tell him, "Do not say, 'I am only a child' . . . Do not be afraid" (Jer 1:7–8).

The earthly father of Jesus, Joseph, was also afraid when confronted with a difficult situation. Mary, his wife-to-be, was already pregnant, even though their marriage had not yet been consummated. An angel of the Lord had to tell Joseph, "Do not be afraid."

The high priest Zechariah was afraid (Luke 1:13) and so was John, the author of the book of Revelation. John tells us in Revelation 1:17, "When I saw him, I fell at his feet as though dead. Then he placed his right hand on me and said, 'Do not be afraid.'"

"Do not be afraid." Why are these words repeated so often in the Bible? This is simply because people in the Bible often found themselves afraid. This also explains why one of the most common descriptions of God in the Psalms is "refuge" or "rock." People found themselves in trouble, and they wanted to hide.[1] Fear is a common experience in the Bible. God's people, including leaders, prophets, priests, and apostles, often felt afraid. Fear is a very common experience not only in the Bible, but even today.

When Typhoon Ondoy flooded Manila and I saw with my own eyes how fast the water rose, I was afraid. That was just water from a flood. How much more the tsunami that devastated parts of northern Japan in 2011?

People are fearful. We just don't want to admit it because we think it is not OK to be afraid. We feel that when we are afraid, we are violating the

---

1. James Limburg, "Book of Psalms," *Anchor Bible Dictionary*, vol. 5 (Garden City, NY: Doubleday, 1992), 535.

command "do not fear" in the Bible. And so we try our best not to be afraid, not to show fear even when we are already afraid.

What "do not be afraid" really means

When God says "do not be afraid," it is not like the other commandments in the Bible, like "do not murder" or "do not steal." If we look at the places in the Bible where these four words occur, we will find that they were given in situations where God's people needed assurance of God's presence or some form of encouragement (for some examples, see Gen 46:3; Deut 20:1; 31:6; Josh 11:6; Isa 44:8; Jer 1:8). Indeed, we can say the words "do not fear" are equivalent to the words "I am here."

When God says "do not fear," he is not giving a command; he is encouraging his people. He is not rebuking his people or scolding them for being afraid. He knows and understands that they are afraid. God knows we are but dust, and are limited. That is why we find passages that contain the encouragement "do not fear" without any reference to the people being afraid (for example, Gen 15:1; 21:17; Num 14:9; John 14:27). When God says to us, "do not be afraid," he is telling us, "I understand what you are going through. I know you are afraid. But don't be. I am here."

To be afraid, therefore, is not in itself a sign of weak faith. To be afraid is, in some sense, "good" because we open up ourselves to God's help and to that of others as well. Sometimes when I am about to preach, I tell my wife, "I'm afraid, I'm nervous. I don't think I can make it." And she tells me, "That's a good sign."

Where fear brings us

We usually think the best position is the position of power, of being in control. But the best position is actually the position of need, for it is when we are not in control, when we feel helpless, that we have more opportunity to experience the power of God. But how can we experience God's power when we are not willing to admit our limitations?

It is when we deny our fear that we shut the door to God and to others. As psychologist Henry Cloud explains:

> Denying fear keeps us out of touch with our humble position in the universe and keeps us away from God. It is our fear and lack of control over much of life that leads us to our heavenly Father;

we must be in touch with our fears to get to a position of need ...
Fear gets us in touch with our very real vulnerability, and it gets
us in touch with our need for others and God. Many times people
treat others very insensitively because they are warding off their
fears of being vulnerable.[2]

That is one reason why we are afraid to admit we are down, to admit we
are sad. That is why some people do not cry – they want to show they are
strong. To admit we are afraid is to say we do not have control, so we fight
against our fear. For example, some men won't even admit they do not know
the directions to a certain place. So they drive their car around for hours,
pretending they know where they are going, when simply asking someone for
directions would have brought them to their destination much earlier.

How to deal with fear

Fear can be a sign of pride, of an "I know it all" or "I don't need your help"
attitude. We can, of course, also go to the other extreme of always confessing
we are afraid and living our lives in fear every moment of the day. This
happens when we do not deal with our fear.

How then do we deal with our fear?

Rather than denying our fear, it is important for us to admit our feelings
of fear to the Lord. Rather than acting as if we are in control of a situation, let
us admit that things are beyond our control and that we are afraid. Let us then
bring to the situation to the Lord. God knows us as we are and understands
every entanglement we go through. He is very willing to journey with us in
any fearful experience we may have – even "through the valley of the shadow
of death."

Wasn't David the one who said, "Even though I walk through the valley of
the shadow of death, I will fear no evil, for you are with me; your rod and your
staff, they comfort me" (Ps 23:4)? David was also the one who courageously
killed Goliath, wasn't he? Yet, amazingly, we also find the following words
ascribed to him:

My heart is in anguish within me; the terrors of death assail me.
Fear and trembling have beset me; horror has overwhelmed me.
I said, "Oh, that I had the wings of a dove! I would fly away and

---

2. Henry Cloud, *Changes That Heal: How to Understand Your Past to Ensure a Healthier Future* (Grand Rapids, MI: Zondervan, 1990; 1992), 201.

be at rest – I would flee far away and stay in the desert; I would hurry to my place of shelter, far from the tempest and storm." (Ps 55:4–8)

David was a great and courageous leader who was not afraid to admit that he was afraid: "The terrors of death assail me. Fear and trembling have beset me." He trembled like I did during the film showing many years ago. But because he acknowledged that he was afraid, he became open to his need for God. That is why at the beginning of this psalm David says to the Lord, "Listen to my prayer, O God, do not ignore my plea; hear me and answer me. My thoughts trouble me and I am distraught" (Ps 55:1–2). He tells God, "Fear and trembling have come upon me." This is what David seems to be saying: "I am so afraid, God. I feel I am going to die." He wishes he could just suddenly vanish and be somewhere else – and he expresses this openly. He says, "Oh, that I had the wings of a dove! I would fly away and be at rest – I would flee far away . . . I would hurry to my place of shelter, far from the tempest and storm" (Ps 55:6–8).

Have you ever felt like that? I have. There have been times in church when I felt I had not done well in my sermon preparation and was preaching terribly. I would find myself wishing that I could just sink into the ground and disappear. I'm sure we have all had experiences like that, including some much more serious ones. But the crucial thing here is that it was when David described or "named" his situation that he was able to move beyond his experience of despair.

I think the metaphor of a dove flying far away speaks of David's own desire. And by being able to express this, he had, in some sense, advanced in his dealing with his fear.

Jacob's story

One of the most moving stories in the book of Genesis is the story of Jacob. He is a man who would do anything to get what he wants. Yet, he is also a man of many fears. Foremost among these is his fear of his brother Esau. Twenty years before, Jacob fled his home because he had fooled his father Isaac into giving him the blessing meant for Esau. When Esau became so angry at this that he wanted to kill Jacob, Jacob fled. For twenty years, he lived with his uncle Laban. During that time, he married Leah and Rachel and accumulated some wealth. But like many of us who have lived abroad, Jacob felt the need to go back home. And so he proceeded to make his way back to his father's land.

But going back meant confronting old issues. And this was not easy. Jacob knew he would have to face Esau – the person he feared. And one memorable night, Jacob heard a report that Esau was coming towards him with four hundred men. Jacob was really afraid then! Rather than denying his fear, however, he admitted it. He went to God and prayed one of the longest prayers in Genesis:

> Then Jacob prayed, "O God of my father Abraham, God of my father Isaac, O LORD, who said to me, 'Go back to your country and your relatives, and I will make you prosper,' I am unworthy of all the kindness and faithfulness you have shown your servant. I had only my staff when I crossed this Jordan, but now I have become two groups. Save me, I pray, from the hand of my brother Esau, *for I am afraid* he will come and attack me, and also the mothers with their children." (Gen 32:9–11, emphasis mine)

For men like Jacob and David to admit "I am afraid" is really something. It's not a sign of weakness. Far from it. On the contrary, such an admission is a sign of courage – both men were able to confront their fear by admitting it. I think this is one thing pastors, church workers, and members of the community of faith should learn – to admit and say, "I am afraid."

Bring your fears to God

The amazing thing is that when we go to the Lord in prayer, acknowledge our fear, and confront it by giving it a name, God opens our eyes. We are made able to see the one who has really been in control of everything all along. David later declared in Psalm 55:19, "God, who is enthroned forever, will hear them and afflict them . . ." In the same way that in Psalm 57 he was able to sing, "Be exalted, O God, above the heavens," so here in Psalm 55 he gets a glimpse of the Lord's power. He is in control. God is still on his throne.

Part of the reason why we are afraid is because we feel we no longer have any control. So some of us become control freaks. We cannot rest until everything is sorted, until there are no more loose ends. In the end, however, we can never actually rest because there will always be something beyond our control. It's different with the Lord. He is the one who is in control. And it is only when we learn to acknowledge our fear in his presence and learn to trust him that we experience his rest and his peace.

The day after the film showing, I cried out to the Lord and struggled to find the words for my fear – struggled to name it and confront it before him. God spoke to me through the very words found in Psalm 55:19: "God, who is enthroned forever, will hear them and afflict them." I started to see a vision of God as one who is in control, the one who is "enthroned." God was telling me that day, "I am still in control. Do not be afraid. I am here." It is not surprising that one of the last verses of Psalm 55 contains the words cited later in 1 Peter 5:7: "Cast your cares on the LORD and he will sustain you" (Ps 55:22). And like what happened to Paul (Acts 9), the mist fell from my eyes and I began to see things not from my perspective but from God's perspective. My situation did not change that day, but something happened within me. My fear met God's presence.

Curiously, after the encouraging words in Psalm 55:22, "Cast your cares on the LORD," we find in the following verse these words: "But you, O God, will bring down the wicked into the pit of corruption; bloodthirsty and deceitful men will not live out half their days. But as for me, I trust in you" (Ps 55:23).

The struggle continues. And it is OK.

Encountering a psalm

Read Psalm 55.

- Some say that because we are Christians, we should no longer be afraid. Do you agree? Are there fears that can be considered "normal"? When does fear become wrong?
- People are afraid of different things. What are you afraid of?
- What can we learn from Psalm 55 about how to deal with our fears?
- One of the blessings in the Psalms is that in this book, God not only gives us his Word, but he also gives us words we can utter to him when we are afraid. If you are afraid right now, try praying aloud the words of Psalm 55:1–8, 16–19.
- How do you balance trusting in God and the reality of the experience of fear? When can we say that we are no longer trusting God in our fear?
- If you are asked to preach from Psalm 55, what would be your main point? How would you go about preparing your outline? (For help in doing this, see the Appendix.)

7

It's OK to Struggle

L ife's really difficult here," the taxi driver was telling me. "No matter how hard you try and how much you work, still nothing happens." He was complaining about how little money he made as a taxi driver. He argued with me about what the fare should be, explaining that the taxi meter was used only within the main Manila area. Outside that area, he explained, the fare is fixed depending on where you live; and I live outside Manila. I told him that was not what the person at the airport had told me.

"Oh, the guy working there is new," he said. "That's why he doesn't know. Anyway, because you were not informed, let's just follow the taxi meter reading."

I was relieved, though the stress of not being sure how much the fare really was made me feel more tired. At least three times during the one-hour drive to my house, the driver repeated his explanation of how much the fare should be and how difficult life is.

I can identify with the taxi driver. As I write this, I am also struggling with financial uncertainties. During a meeting yesterday, the president of our seminary informed us that we will get our salary only up to the middle of next month. After that, we will no longer be paid. That's less than a month left! Where will I get the money to pay my children's tuition? Where will I get the money to make the payments on our house and to meet our basic needs? I was not able to sleep last night, thinking about what our situation will be like and praying all the while.

We all struggle in life

The sad reality is that many of us struggle financially. A recent survey shows that the rate of unemployment in the Philippines rose to more than 27.2

percent in 2011 from 2010's 23.5 percent. That's about 11.3 million Filipinos who are jobless.[1] When I read this, I found it difficult to continue what I was doing. If those of us who have jobs are struggling, how much more those who do not have jobs? Many of us are *"isang kahig, isang tuka,"* living hand-to-mouth, earning just enough to feed ourselves for a day at a time, and that often just barely. No insurance. No savings. Nothing. Just what you need for the day. What about the other important things in life like health and education? What happens when someone in the family gets sick? This is one of the major reasons why more than 10 percent of Filipinos are now working abroad.

Yet those of us who get the chance to work or live abroad soon discover that those who live in richer countries are struggling too. They may be rich but they are not happy. Just recently a movement was launched in the UK called the "Happiness Movement." People living in First World countries are realizing that money can't buy happiness. According to one report, "levels of well-being in Britain, the United States and other countries remained static even as disposable income and financial security soared during the great postwar expansion of Western economies." What this is saying is that even during those most productive years, people's levels of happiness did not improve. Those who lived in poor countries like Bangladesh and Nigeria were even found to be "ahead of much richer European and North American nations" in terms of what British Prime Minister David Cameron called "general well-being." He said, "It's time we focused not just on GDP but on GWB – general well-being."[2]

Loneliness, depression, and emptiness are serious problems that some of the rich struggle with, especially in First World countries. When we were living in the UK, my daughter came home one day, saying, "Dad, many of my classmates were crying this morning at the start of our class. Even the teacher was crying with them."

"Why were they crying?" her mom and I asked.

"Because most of my classmates' parents are divorced," she said. One of her classmates had been sharing how her dad had just walked away that morning and told them he was not coming back. The class had talked about it, and their teacher shared that she herself came from a broken home.

---

1. *Manila Bulletin*, 23 May 2011 (http://www.mb.com.ph, accessed 3 June 2011).

2. *Philippine Daily Inquirer*, 14 April 2011. The caption to the article reads, *"Diyan angat ang pinoy, kahit mahirap masaya"* [That's where Filipinos are better; they are happy even though they are poor]. See http://newsinfo.inquirer.net/3146/happiness-movement-starts-with-lotsa-hugs, accessed 24 Aug 2016.

Even some things we take for granted here can be a big issue in richer countries. Sleep, for example. When I visited Singapore, I saw that a church was advertising a talk on how to deal with sleep problems and urging people to register for it. I found myself thinking, *sleep problems must be a big issue here if they can be used to attract people to come to church. And they even have such a thing as an expert on sleep!* I have also seen on the Internet that there is a National Center on Sleep Disorders in the USA. That's unheard of in the Philippines, where the problem is more likely to be where to sleep rather than how to sleep. We have places in Manila where there is so little room in the house that the occupants have to schedule their sleep. For instance, someone will sleep from 7 p.m. till 12 a.m. Then he or she will have to get up because another will need the place for the 12 a.m. to 5 a.m. "shift." The physical space may be very small, but at least people here can sleep once they lie down!

The reality is that both the rich and the poor have struggles in life. Some struggle with poverty and material suffering; others with emotional and psychological issues. While some may argue that one is better than the other, the point is that we all struggle with something. The dictionary defines the verb "to struggle" as "to make a hard effort to deal with a challenge or problem or difficulty." In that sense all of us are struggling. We all have a hard time with something or some things. We all struggle.

Some of you may ask, *"Hindi ba pwedeng walang struggles?"* [Isn't it possible to have no struggles?] I wish the answer were "yes." I wish I could wake up one day not worrying about how and where to get enough money to pay my children's tuition. I wish I could wake up every morning happy and refreshed, with no worries or dark moods. I wish I did not have to struggle with my own weaknesses. But we know it's only those buried six feet below the ground who do not have struggles. We say in the Philippines, *"Habang may buhay, may pagasa"* [As long as there is life, there is hope]. In the same way, we also know that *"Habang may buhay, may struggles"* [as long as there is life, there are struggles].

When God's people struggle financially

When we open our Bibles we discover that even God's people struggle. They are also crying, "But I am poor and needy; hasten to me, O God! You are my help and my deliverer, O LORD, do not delay!" (Ps 70:5 ESV). A Filipino could very well compose those words. Whenever I ask our people in the church what their prayer requests are during our praying meetings, the most common petition I hear is "for a financial problem." Hearing the words of the psalmist makes us realize we are not alone. Many of God's people are also poor. Yet it is because they are poor and very much in need that they come to God asking for his mercy and help.

When we are in a situation of need, we have more opportunity to cry out to God. When you work very hard and still nothing happens, then you have more opportunity to depend on God and in the process, experience his power. You know in your heart what the psalmist is speaking about when he says, "The eyes of all look to you, and you give them their food at the proper time" (Ps 145:15). We know how the psalmist feels when he says, "I lift up my eyes to the hills – where does my help come from? My help comes from the LORD, the Maker of heaven and earth" (Ps 121:1–2).

I remember the story of two women who went to speak to their spiritual director; one was rich, the other was poor. The poor one spoke first. She complained, "Life's really hard. She seems to be having it so much better because she is rich." Then the rich woman's turn came. She told the spiritual director, "I envy that lady," referring to the poor woman, "she prays so intensely, it's almost like she can touch God."

When Gracia Burnham went back to the USA after she was rescued from the Abu Sayyaf in Mindanao, she was asked by a reporter, "What is the difference between life in the jungle under your captors and your life now that you're back in the USA?" This was her answer: "Here when you are thirsty you just open the faucet, and there is water. If you are hungry you just open the fridge and get something to munch. But in the mountains, when you are thirsty, you cry out to God."

I remember going home one day and feeling bewildered at the sight of my daughter extending her hand inside our fridge. The fridge was open and there was nothing inside. Well, that's not entirely true; there was water in there, lots of water. I asked my daughter what she was doing. She told me she was praying for God to give us food. I will never forget her prayers during those times; they were like the words of the psalmist: "Out of the depths I cry to you, O LORD" (Ps 130:1).

We struggle with emotional problems

"Out of the depths I cry to you, O LORD" is one of the prayers in the Psalms that resonates with our own experience, not only when we struggle with material problems but also when we struggle with emotional problems, with our inner pain and suffering. People from other backgrounds may have problems different from the ones we face, but they also know what it is like to deeply struggle. My former seminary teacher from Canada tells us that in his country you can see villages that look OK on the outside. The residents don't have problems with money; they are super-rich compared to most of us. But scratch a little beneath the surface and you will see some really serious problems like alcoholism, drug addiction, and child abuse. The people are just tired, bored, and dying inside.

The Bible speaks also of emotional struggles. Tired and spilled out, David cries, "I am worn out from groaning; all night long I flood my bed with weeping and drench my couch with tears" (Ps 6:6). He can identify with the words of another psalmist, "My tears have been my food day and night" (Ps 42:3). Have there been times in your life when you have experienced the same? You would go home and wish you had a place where you could just cry. You would stay awake all night crying. David's experience was not a one-time event. He also tells us how he struggled with sadness and sorrow, how he struggled with his thoughts: "How long must I wrestle with my thoughts and every day have sorrow in my heart?" (Ps 13:2). In Filipino we would say, "*Siguro napapraning na siya*" [Maybe he is losing his mind]. After thinking and thinking about a problem, many of us have experienced feeling as if our minds are overused and tired. It was the same with David as he kept thinking of how to solve his problems. He felt sad and tired, and he complained, "How long?" He repeats these words a number of times.

When people during ancient times asked "How long?" they were referring to a really long time, unlike today when two minutes is already too long when we are in front of our computers. "How long?" in ancient times meant years, not just days or weeks.

But people in the Bible don't just give up. They keep on trying, just like the psalmist in Psalm 42/43 who repeats his prayer three times: "*Why are you downcast, O my soul? . . . Put your hope in God, for I will yet praise him, my Savior and my God*" (Pss 42:5, 11; 43:5). When the psalmist repeats his prayer, he is showing his struggle with finding inner peace, as well as his perseverance in seeking it.

Do you sometimes feel like that? You feel sad and lonely. You hope it will go away. But after a while you realize the sadness and loneliness are still there. You go to church. Everyone is singing happy and joyful songs, but you find it hard to join in. The songs sound almost strange to you, not touching your soul at all.

You hear people in church say, "When you don't feel like praising God, you should praise him more." So you try to praise the Lord with all your might. But you know you can't fool yourself forever. It's not that you are bad or that you lack faith. It's just that, no matter how much you try, you still feel that same darkness hovering over you. You tell yourself, *I want to praise the Lord because God loves me. So I should praise the Lord no matter what.* You try doing this a number of times. But after some time you stop trying and you just sit down.

I have heard of a Christian in Australia who, in the middle of the worship time, shouted "I feel like Psalm 88!" Psalm 88 is one of the darkest psalms (we will talk about it in ch. 8). We would not do that in the Philippines. We are shy people and we do not want to stand out. But if we were to be honest, many of us would admit that we are enduring deep and painful struggles.

I have experienced this. I would go to church and the singing would go on and on, and I would struggle to identify with the message of the songs. I would struggle even more on the days when I had to preach, because after the singing it would be my turn. One time, I was asked to preach on Easter Sunday. I told my spiritual director afterwards that I had felt like Good Friday even as I preached a resurrection message. It was torment.

We struggle with the will of God, just as Jesus did

I'm glad I am not alone in my struggles. We are not alone. Jesus struggled too. During his most difficult hour he prayed to his Father, "*Father, if it is possible, let this cup pass away from me; But not my will but your will be done*" (Matt 26:39). Interestingly, like the psalmist in Psalm 42/43, Jesus repeats this prayer three times. He was about to face suffering and death, which he described as his "cup." He brought his three closest friends (Peter, James, and John) with him, just as we want our closest friends with us when we go through really difficult situations. But Jesus had to leave his friends for a while to utter this prayer (there are paths only we can tread; not even our friends can join us). The first time Jesus prayed, "Father, if it is possible, let this cup pass away from me. But not my will but your will be done," you would think the matter had been settled. He returned to his disciples, however, found them sleeping, and then left them again, went back on his knees and prayed the same prayer. And then all this happened once more – three times in total. You can almost picture Jesus walking to and fro, repeatedly getting up and then kneeling down with his face to the ground. He was having a really hard time. He was struggling.

We like to think of Jesus facing his suffering peacefully and joyfully. There is an element of this, of course. Hebrews 12:2 tells us that Jesus "for the joy set before him endured the cross, scorning its shame, and sat down at the right hand of the throne of God." But we also know Jesus struggled. And this in spite of the fact that Jesus knew he was fulfilling the purpose for which he was sent. In Jesus's prayer at Gethsemane, it was as if he was telling his Father:

> Father, I know we have talked about this in eternity. I have agreed to be the Lamb to be slaughtered for the sins of humanity. Recently, I have even prayed that you would be glorified through my death in the same way that I have glorified you through my ministry (John 17:1). But to be honest about it, it's really hard. In fact, right now, I wish I did not have to walk this path.

Even as he adds in the end, "Not my will but your will be done," Jesus had a really hard time. This may shock some Christians who always equate maturity of faith to the absence of struggles. I know of one Christian leader who suffered immensely and never complained. The members of his church said they felt blessed because their leader had faced his suffering with peace and joy. But this is not true for everyone. The good news is that when we suffer, we do not have to force ourselves to be joyful or serene; it's OK to struggle. The Bible tells us that Jesus has been tempted just like us (Heb 4:15). And for many people, knowing this is a great encouragement.

> For we do not have a high priest who is unable to sympathize with our weaknesses, but we have one who has been tempted in every way, just as we are – yet was without sin.

Because he has gone through the same experience, Jesus is able to sympathize with us in our weaknesses.

We struggle with our weaknesses

The Apostle Paul reveals how he struggled with a weakness he had, which he calls his "thorn in the flesh." The image of a "thorn" indicates this is something negative, like the negative emotions we have been talking about. It is something we would not want to have if we had a choice. So difficult was this "thorn" for Paul that he actually prayed for it to be taken away. Like the psalmist and Jesus, Paul prayed three times about his "thorn in the flesh."

Clearly, Paul was really desperate. To pray for something three times implies that one has exhausted all the possible means of finding relief. To repeat one's prayer three times also shows that the person is struggling, as we have seen in the case of Jesus and the psalmist.

We know from his other letters that Paul asked for prayer (Eph 6:19–20) and prayed for others as well (Phil 1:4; 1 Thess 1:2). But this is the only occasion where Paul tells us he prayed for something three times. Each time, Paul tells us his prayer was turned down. The Lord, instead, answered Paul by telling him that his grace is sufficient, "for my power is made perfect in weakness" (2 Cor 12:9). In the end, Paul concedes that all this has been for his own good, in order that God's power may be declared through his weakness. Knowing the purpose of his suffering may have lessened Paul's torment, but the reason for his struggles remained unknown to him. Paul died a struggling apostle.

Paul's experience shows that some struggles are for life. Some struggles, of course, can be remedied or if not, lessened. For instance, if a sin is causing our struggle, confession of our sin and changing our ways can allow us to experience freedom. But there are struggles that will have to wait until we get to eternity to be sorted out.

Why we still struggle

But wait a minute, some may argue, why do we still have to struggle? Are we not already justified by faith? Didn't Paul tell us that "there is now no condemnation for those who are in Christ" (Rom 8:1)? Jesus has already paid the price for our sins. Didn't he declare on the cross, "It is finished"? So why do we still have to struggle? Many of us can't understand what place struggles have in a life that has already been redeemed by the blood of Christ.

Some will say, "*Tapos na ang laban*" [the fight is over]. It's like watching Manny Pacquiao[3] on delayed telecast or replay. We already know he has won, so there is no need for us to be tense. We can be quite relaxed as we watch the fight, eating peanuts, with our feet up on the table and with cheering in the room. Even if we see Pacquiao struggling, cornered and appearing to be having a hard time, we do not worry because we already know he has won. In the same way, these people reason, we know God has already won the ultimate battle, so we no longer have to struggle.

---

3. Manny Pacquiao is, as of this writing, the world's pound-for-pound king and the only boxer in history to win eight world titles in eight different weight divisions.

I agree there is a connection between the boxing illustration and our experience as believers, for indeed we know and believe that God wins at the end. But there is a difference between watching a Manny Pacquiao fight and living the Christian life. For one, the end has not yet come; no one among us has actually seen what will transpire at the end of time. Even the Apostle John, who wrote the book of Revelation, can only use images to describe to us what was revealed to him. Words falter when we begin to describe the end, so it's not like we are watching it on replay. We know God has won, but we do not know and understand exactly how and when. That is why even the martyred people of God in the book of Revelation cry out to the Lord, "How long?" (Rev 6:10). We know God wins in the end, but our life in the meantime is certainly not struggle-free. It takes a lot of faith. We do not even know what our resurrection body will look like, for none of us have been resurrected yet.

A bigger difference is that, unlike in the boxing analogy, Christians are not the ones in front of the TV, watching the fight transpire. We are right there inside the ring, fighting for our life. We know God wins in the end. But there are times when we feel like that's not true anymore because we are being beaten and pushed back, and we fall while the crowd is shouting at us, taunting us. Is it really true that we will win in the end? We believe so. But for the moment, we feel like we are being devastated.

Some of us don't feel like the winning Pacquiao. We feel more like his opponent, with our faces swollen and bruised, our bodies reeling from the heavy blows we are receiving. Similarly, the church is bombarded on all sides with tragedies of immorality, injustice, sufferings, and exploitation. We know God wins in the end. But there are times – and for some the time may be now – when we don't see that end coming. Some people even wonder if believers will ever truly win. One British Anglican once told me, "I wish God were more visible and active in his church today."

We only see glimpses of his power and presence. In some parts of the world it is God's absence that is felt. Christians are a minority. They are marginalized, persecuted, excommunicated. When Bin Laden died, for example, Christians in Pakistan found themselves utterly ostracized. Some of their own people thought, and continue to think, that they had a part in his killing. People outside their country also do not trust them.

In places where the church is richer and more influential, Christians have a different kind of struggle – they wrestle with living as "rich Christians in an age of hunger." What's more, they struggle to maintain their unity, harmony, and purity. Their temptations and problems may be of a different quality, but they are just as great.

And so like the psalmist we call to God from the depths (Ps 42 – "deep calls to deep"). We feel overwhelmed, not knowing where to go and what to do. We sometimes wonder whether this struggling, small bunch of God's people will really come out victorious one day. We believe we will. In the parable of the mustard seed, Jesus said that the kingdom of God on earth will one day be like a big tree, one whose branches are broad enough for birds of all kinds to build their nests there.

The tension between future glory and present suffering

But that victory will happen "one day." For now, we are caught "between the times." We are in the midst of the tension between what we should be because of the dawning of the age to come resulting from Christ's coming to earth, and the present reality in which we find ourselves. The glory of the coming kingdom dawned when Jesus came to earth. But it is not yet completely here. It will only be when he comes again to earth in his glory. This makes us a people of future glory and at the same time, of present suffering. We are simultaneously a people of the cross and of the resurrection. We have already within us the firstfruits of eternity, yet we bear in our bodies the marks of suffering.

We often think life may have been easier for New Testament believers – and perhaps, for us today – for the early Christians already had their hope in Jesus Christ. In Old Testament times, people did not have the promise of eternal life. Our real situation as believers, however, regardless of when we live, is similar to the experience of the Shunammite woman in 2 Kings 4. She was childless when the prophet Elisha met her. Although her situation was far from ideal, she had learned to accept her lot. So when Elisha told her she would have a son the following year, she said to him, "No, my LORD . . . don't mislead your servant" (2 Kgs 4:16b). But true to the word of God through the prophet, the woman did get pregnant and bore a child. It must have been a great time of celebration when such a miracle took place. But a few years later, the child died. This created even more agony for the woman than her suffering from being childless. So she told Elisha, "Did I ask you for a son, my LORD? Didn't I tell you, 'Don't raise my hopes'?" (2 Kgs 4:28).

As believers, our hopes have indeed been raised because of the coming of Jesus Christ. But for some of us who are going through extreme difficulties, the promises of future glory can feel like a big contradiction. Thoughts of the promised future glory can become a tormenting experience when suffering believers realize what a huge gap there is between the promised glory and their present experience. Of course, the future glory can bring hope to those who are suffering (Rom 8:18), but such hope and comfort cannot be said to be readily felt and available all the time. Especially for those undergoing severe emotional pain (like depression) or extreme persecution and loss, the tension between the future and the present can become so great that they can't help but cry out, "How long, LORD? Will you forget me forever?" (Ps 13:1). Those of us who minister to the suffering and those of us who suffer would do well to remember this point.

Just like the friends of Job, we can commit the mistake of offering advice and explanations rather than just sitting beside our friends to listen to them and allow them to express their pain. I feel it may help a little if we understand more about the nature of the life of faith, which involves struggles of the most intense and difficult kind – even for believers. Rather than offering false hopes to friends who are suffering, we can present them with the reality. For it is only by confronting our reality that we experience freedom. As spiritual director and writer Thomas Merton explains: "True faith is never merely a source of spiritual comfort. It may indeed bring peace, but before it does so it must involve us in struggle. A 'faith' that avoids this struggle is really a temptation against true faith."[4]

We are still in the process of being changed

Another reason why believers struggle is because, in the midst of the tension we are in, we are already in the process of moving towards the future glory. This movement, as Merton explains, involves a struggle because we go through a process. We know that even though we have already been justified by faith, we are still in the process of being changed. Spiritual writer Robert Mulholland says, "Spiritual formation is a process of being conformed to the image of Christ for the sake of others."[5] Unfortunately, we do not like being in a process. A process involves steps. It requires time. In fact, it can be frustratingly slow – and some Christians want to grow really fast. The monk

---

4. Thomas Merton, *New Seeds of Contemplation* (London: Burns & Oates, 1962, 1999), 78.

5. M. Robert Mulholland Jr., *Invitation to a Journey: A Road Map for Spiritual Formation* (Downers Grove, IL: InterVarsity Press, 1993), 15.

and writer Brother Lawrence once complained of a certain nun, describing her as one who "wants to grow faster than grace allows."[6]

Some Christians wish there were some kind of capsule, a spiritual one, which they could take and then all their struggles would be gone! They wish there were some kind of prayer of deliverance that could be uttered by a spiritual leader, a prayer that could free them from all weaknesses. But how many pastors have prayed for our weaknesses, and yet we continue to struggle? How many seminars and conferences have we attended, hoping to find the promised resolution and release from our weaknesses, only to be confronted with the same issues? Some Christian groups actually think that all it takes to free a struggling believer from all troubles is some ritual of deliverance, and then everything will be OK. In such rituals you literally vomit your weaknesses or whatever struggle you have. In other groups you sweat them out. I sometimes wonder, though, how many times a believer has to go through such "vomiting" sessions.

Processes of growth are part of the life of faith. How quickly we turn from being a spiritual giant to being an ugly sinner! You have just attended a spiritual retreat and really feel on fire for God. Then your son annoys you, and suddenly your zeal for God is gone. You still burn with fire, but it's no longer godly fire. I remember my teacher in seminary saying, "When you become a parent, you realize you are really a sinner."

How often do we feel frustrated that even after years of being a believer, we still struggle with the same old issues? Spiritual writer Henri Nouwen, whose writings have touched many lives, admitted that he still struggled with the same issues twenty-nine years after his ordination. He confessed: "Looking back, I realize that I am still struggling with the same problems I had on the day of my ordination twenty-nine years ago . . . Very little, if anything, has changed with regard to my search for inner unity and peace. I am still the restless, nervous, intense, distracted, and impulse-driven person I was when I set out on this spiritual journey."[7]

Why are we like this?

It is because although we have already been changed as a result of our union with Christ, the process of change has not yet been completed. We know from 2 Corinthians 5:17 that we have already been changed: "If anyone

---

6. Brother Lawrence, *The Practice of the Presence of God* (Mount Vernon, NY: Peter Pauper Press, 1963).

7. Wil Hernandez, *Henri Nouwen: A Spirituality of Imperfection* (New York: Paulist Press, 2006), 102.

is in Christ, he is a new creation; the old has gone, behold, the new has come." Yet Paul also tells us that this change is still ongoing: "And we all, with unveiled face, beholding the glory of the Lord, are being transformed into the same image from one degree of glory to another" (2 Cor 3:18 ESV). Notice that the tense of the verb is not simple past ("were transformed"), but present progressive ("being transformed"), meaning it is an ongoing process. We are not yet fully changed; we are still in process.

The passage in Colossians 3:9–10 is more illuminating:

> Do not lie to each other, since you have taken off your old self with its practices and have put on the new self, which is being renewed in knowledge in the image of its Creator.

Paul tells us that as believers we have already "put on the new self." So it is already new. But he goes on to describe the nature of this "new self." He says that this new self is "being renewed." God is not yet finished with us.[8]

God is not yet finished with us. As John Calvin writes: "Creatures of such instability, and liable to be borne away by a thousand different influences, we need to be confirmed again and again."[9] Like Paul's experience in Romans 7, there are times when we like to do the right thing but end up doing the very thing we do not want to do.[10] Paul writes: "I do not understand what I do. For what I want to do I do not do, but what I hate I do" (Rom 7:15).

I am not encouraging complacency here. Far from it. As Christians, we need to keep on living holy lives, by God's grace, and grow in our walk with God. This explains the numerous exhortations in the Bible urging believers to live as God has called them (e.g. Rom 12:1–2; Eph 4:1). At the same time, however, we need to be careful we do not go to the extent where we think we are not doing well whenever we fail. Perfectionism, according to one spiritual writer, is one of the biggest hindrances to the life of faith: "For us there is only the trying, one step at a time . . . Perfectionism, willful striving for spiritual achievement and expectation of complete spiritual wholeness are major obstacles to the spiritual journey."[11] As I have written elsewhere:

---

8. Or as we say in Tagalog, "*Hindi pa tapos ang Diyos sa atin.*"

9. Calvin, *Commentary on the Book of Psalms*, trans. J. Anderson (Edinburgh: Edinburgh Printing, 1846), 423.

10. As one Filipino song says, "*Gusto kong bumait pero 'di ko magawa*" (I want to behave better but I just can't do it).

11. Richard Byrne, "Journey, Growth and Development in Spiritual Life," in *The New Dictionary of Catholic Spirituality*, ed. Michael Downey (Collegeville, MN: Liturgical Press, 1993).

Human life remains very much a process. Indeed, to be human is to be partial, incomplete, undone. We cry for help and get help. Yet the next time around we are back on our knees, pleading for mercy that God deliver us. And it is only in our ability to live with grace in our own imperfections that healing flows.[12]

Struggling like Jacob

Inevitably we will all struggle. We are like Jacob in the Old Testament. Jacob, we can say, was a born struggler. Even before he came out of his mother's womb, he was already struggling with his twin brother Esau. That was why he was called *supplanter* (Gen 25:26). Jacob struggled with himself. He struggled with his fear. As we have seen in the previous chapter, Jacob admitted to God that he was afraid (Gen 32:11). He struggled with the issue of control. He had just prayed and asked for help from God, but the next thing we know, he was orchestrating his own schemes to make sure he stayed safe. He was about to meet his brother again after twenty years, but then he was told that Esau was coming to him with four hundred men (Gen 32:6). We can imagine Jacob trembling with fear. He therefore thought of a strategy involving the proper "arrangement" of his men, including gifts to be given to Esau. Next, he risked the lives of his own family by crossing the River Jabbok by night, which according to some scholars is a fast-flowing river (Gen 32:22–23). Only someone with a disturbed mind would try to cross it at night.[13]

Given what Jacob had done many years back – getting the blessing meant for Esau through deception – we can understand why he was so afraid. He was someone who constantly struggled with other people. He struggled with his brother and later with his uncle. But what is most remarkable about this man is that he not only struggled with himself and with other people, he also struggled with God. In that enigmatic encounter between Jacob and a heavenly being (Gen 32:22–32), whom the narrator later identifies as God himself, we see Jacob as the ultimate struggler.

We would think that as Jacob grew older, his struggles would decrease. On the contrary, Jacob's struggles actually intensified as his journey progressed. The first time God revealed himself to him was in a dream while

---

12. Villanueva, "Preaching Lament," in *Reclaiming the Old Testament for Christian Preaching*, eds. Grenville J. R. Kent, Paul J. Kissling, and Laurence A. Turner (Downers Grove, IL: IVP Academic, 2010), 76.

13. Gordon J. Wenham, *Genesis 16–50* (Dallas, TX: Word Books, 1994), 292.

he was asleep. It was quiet and serene. The next time Jacob encountered God – many years later – he was wide awake. This encounter was far from serene; here, Jacob struggled with God himself. For many of us, the more we grow in our relationship with God, the more challenging life seems and the deeper our struggles feel. Struggles take on subtler forms as we progress in the faith. There is no holding back for the faithful. We struggle with fear, with experiences of being down. We feel sad and cry. Like Jacob, we struggle with others, with issues of anger and rebellion. And we struggle with God. But in all our struggles, as we learned in the previous chapters, we do not retreat. We face our struggles. We face our fears. We admit our struggles with emotional and financial problems. More importantly, we come to God with our struggles. Just like Jacob, we struggle with God. And in his presence we are transformed, for we are not to let go until God blesses us.

Encountering a psalm

Read Psalm 13.

- In our psalm we read: "How long must I wrestle with my thoughts and every day have sorrow in my heart? How long will my enemy triumph over me?" (Ps 13:2). Can you identify with the psalmist's experience? Have there been times in your life when you have really prayed for something for a long time and yet you have not received the answer?
- Some Christians think that because they are already in Christ, there will be no more struggles. What do you think about this?
- Why do you think we continue to struggle as believers?
- What are your struggles right now? Financial? Emotional? Doing the will of God? Weaknesses? Others (name them) _____

    Like the psalmist, try expressing your struggles to the Lord. It may also help to share your struggle(s) with a trusted friend or counselor. When we hide our struggles, they become our dark side.

- While we believe in the reality of our experience of God's deliverance, we also know that this is an ongoing process. How is this process reflected in Psalm 31? Compare especially verses 1–8 and verses 9–18.
- How would you construct a sermon based on Psalm 31? (See Appendix for guide.)

8

It's OK to Be Angry

"You don't become angry with them. Even when they have done wrong to us, we should continue to act in love towards them," Ricar told his wife. "But isn't that hypocrisy?" Ellen blurted out. "No," Ricar answered, "We should continue to show the fruit of the Holy Spirit, no matter how badly other people treat us."

We listened to Ricar as he related how he and Ellen had been trying to deal with a problem in their church. Ricar had been a classmate of mine in Bible school. I had not seen him for more than a decade, so I was really excited when he asked me if I could join him, along with two other classmates, for a time of fellowship. "I just want to share our burden with someone," Ricar now told us. He and Ellen had been back in the Philippines for more than two months. "We are no longer going back to our church in Canada," he said.

For ten years, Ricar and his wife had served in a church in Canada. Under the leadership of a Filipino senior pastor, they had done their best to support this predominantly Filipino community. The first six years had been busy; they had been like the disciples in Mark 6:31 who did not even have the time to eat because of so many people going to and fro. It had been a financially difficult time for them as well. New to Canada, they were constantly adjusting to the high cost of living, and they were not receiving much financially from the church. In spite of all this, Ricar and Ellen served faithfully and endured the hardships. As time passed, their church grew in membership and in finances, and at the end of six years it opened an outreach church in another part of Canada. Ricar and Ellen were sent to pioneer this church. They started from scratch, beginning with only eight members, including the two of them. The next four years were no different from the first six years of their ministry. After these four years, however, their small church had grown to about 200 people. "The Lord blessed the church financially as well," Ricar testified.

Meanwhile, the mother church had been encountering some financial difficulties as it tried to support its growing ministries. Ricar's outreach church soon attracted the attention of his senior pastor. Thinking that this church could be an asset to the mother church, the senior pastor started visiting Ricar's church more often – and Ricar did not find anything unusual about this. While he and Ellen were on vacation in the Philippines, however, the senior pastor took over the leadership of the outreach church. When the couple returned to Canada, the leaders were no longer supportive of them; whenever Ricar made a proposal, they would automatically block it. He at first thought that it was nothing serious; but a series of events made it obvious that there was a deeper problem. Silently and slowly, the couple were being kicked out of the church they had pioneered.

"So we decided to just leave," Ricar shared with us. "Why did you have to leave?" I protested. Ricar explained, "It was better that we leave, because our staying would have created disunity in the church; the important thing was to keep the unity and peace." They had preferred to contain their pain and hurt rather than cause disunity among the church members. And that's what they did. They tried to contain whatever pain they were experiencing just between themselves as husband and wife.

My heart felt heavy as I went home that night. If there is something wrong, one doesn't just walk away. Ricar and Ellen had done nothing wrong, and I felt they should not have left. Would it have been OK for them to be angry – and to express their anger? Did they really have to just keep quiet and walk away?

Dealing with anger

We Filipinos do not usually confront those who have hurt us or done us wrong. We are so concerned with the relationship that we are afraid to express what is really in our hearts. We fear destroying our relationships with others. We just keep what we feel within us, and so, even if we are angry, we do not express it. We would rather "keep the peace." In the meantime, however, we suffer.

Ricar informed us he had had surgery four months prior. The pressure, tension, and all the pain and hurt of the past ten years had taken their toll on him. Unexpressed emotions and repressed anger are really destructive.

Anger can easily lead to violence and hurt; with it, we can destroy others. On the other hand, anger can also destroy us if we don't deal with it properly, just as it did Ricar. How, then, do we deal with anger in such a way that it does not lead to hurting others or ourselves?

We should be honest about what we feel. We need to unload the burden and pain we feel in our hearts. But we don't have to express our anger to the ones who hurt us; at least, not right away. Ricar did the right thing in sharing his burden with us. We must be careful, however, about whom we share our angry feelings with, as few people can actually take it when we share our anger.

Angry psalms

It is here that the lament psalms, especially those we traditionally call the "imprecatory psalms," can be of real help to us. In these psalms, people express their anger to God in a way that is not censured, without any concern about whether they are "showing the fruit of the Spirit" or not. In voicing anger there is openness and honesty, which is often absent in many of our communities.

We'll talk about this further. In the meantime, listen to the following imprecatory psalms:

> Let death take my enemies by surprise; let them go down alive to the grave, for evil finds lodging among them. (Ps 55:15)

> May their eyes be darkened so they cannot see, and their backs be bent forever. (Ps 69:23)

> May they be blotted out of the book of life and not be listed with the righteous. (Ps 69:28)

> I have nothing but hatred for them; I count them my enemies. (Ps 139:22)

Some of you may be shocked at these prayers. Are we not sinning against God when we express our anger this way? You are probably saying, "I do get angry, but I have never wished my enemy dead." Well, maybe not. But honestly – don't we sometimes wish that those who hurt us will just be struck by lightning (as we say in Tagalog, "*Tamaan sana siya ng kidlat!*"). This sounds like the prayer in Psalm 55:15, except that we do not say it out loud. We think we shouldn't. Even when we Christians are very angry, we do not say so – not even to God. In fact, we even say nice things about those who hurt us in front of others and God. We say things like, "O Lord, bless him," even though, in our hearts, we want to call down lightning to strike that person dead.

Hiding our anger from God?

Not admitting to others that we are angry at someone is understandable, though not always right. But hiding our anger from God, telling him we love the one we are angry with, even praying for God to bless him when we really hate that person – who are we fooling? With others, at least, we can hide our anger – they do not know what we really feel. It's like being on social networking sites like Facebook where we can hide our true feelings – even our identities – and project any image of ourselves that we choose. But with God we cannot do that; he knows us through and through. "Before a word is on my tongue," the psalmist tells us, "you know it completely, O LORD" (Ps 139:4). There is nothing we can hide from the Lord. Adam and Eve tried doing that; they hid themselves with leaves, they tried to hide their sin. But God knows.

When we say to the Lord, "Lord, I love my brother/sister. I pray that you bless him/her," and yet, in fact, we feel really angry inside, then isn't that hypocrisy? We know anger is sinful when allowed to go out of control and destroy others. Anger can also be sinful when we keep it too long within us that it turns into bitterness. This too can be destructive, for it destroys the angry person, just like what happened to Ricar. And it can also destroy others, when it bursts just like an erupting volcano. Unexpressed anger will always find a way out.

But anger can also be sinful when we deny it; when we say we are not angry when we actually are. Some Christians will not admit they are angry, even though it is obvious among those around them that they are. These people may be afraid to be angry, thinking that they need to obey the commands of Jesus – for doesn't Jesus command us to "love our enemies," and to "bless those who curse us, to bless and do not curse"? Besides, didn't the Apostle John tell us in 1 John 3:12 and 15 that one who hates his brother is like Cain – that he is a murderer? And who would want to be tagged as a murderer? This is probably one reason why many Christians do not want to admit they are angry; they cannot imagine themselves as murderers. So they hide their anger within them, denying that it exists. This way, they look nice to others and are able to maintain their relationships. They also want to look nice and pious and loving before God, so in their prayers they pray nice things for those who have hurt them. With such people, the problem is deeper than anger; it is pride.

Please don't get me wrong. I am not saying that we need to pray for something bad to happen to others – to pray that our enemies be struck by lightning. What I am saying is that it does not help to be dishonest about what is really in our hearts. God knows what is in our hearts anyway. The very moment we ask God to bless those who have hurt us, the moment we tell him that we love them, God may already be saying, "My dear daughter, I know what is in your heart. It's all right, you can be honest with me." For although we may be telling God nice things about others, we may be doing so with seething eyes and clenched teeth. A better alternative is to go to God and honestly tell him what we feel, including what we want to happen to the person in question. God is not a fool; he will not do the harm that you are asking. He will not send lightning to kill that person. He is a loving and just God, and he knows and understands that we may just be feeling angry at the moment.

It's not so much how God responds that is important here, but it is what happens to us when we are honest with him about what we truly feel. For one thing, we are humbled. Facing your anger is actually a humbling experience, and this is not easy. This is true especially for leaders who are known as models of loving others – it is not easy for them to allow anger. Being honest about our anger with ourselves and with God can be a difficult process, but it is necessary.

The psalms process our anger

Anger management experts advise us that when we are angry, we should take a deep breath and count one to ten to avoid unnecessary violent actions or sudden bursts of anger, the effects of which we will regret. I suggest that when we are angry, we come to God, tell him what is really in our hearts, and tell him what we feel. Maybe we can take a deep breath, and as we do so, we can utter our prayer. Now again, you may ask, *What do I say? How do I pray?* Here, the imprecatory prayers can help us.

The imprecatory psalms help us process our anger. It is important to remember this fact: As believers, we need to be loving. Jesus commands us to love one another. It is by loving one another that the world will know we are his disciples. But we also know that loving others is not easy; it can be a long and difficult process. What do we do when we feel angry with someone we know we are supposed to love? Some Christians may cite the passage in Ephesians 4:26 that says we should not let the sun go down on our anger. So even if we are not OK, are we to just embrace one another and say that we are? That may help momentarily, but we would still need to deal with whatever issue we are facing.

What the lament psalms – the imprecatory psalms in particular – do is they help us process our anger by giving us permission to be angry. The fact that these prayers have been preserved in the Holy Scriptures tells us they are there for a purpose. Otherwise, they would have been stricken out of the Holy Book. These prayers tell us it's OK to be angry. It's OK to express our anger to God.

One of my students reacted when I taught about the imprecatory prayers. He said we should not keep a record of wrongs. What's amazing is that it seems we do have a "record" of wrongs – of words of anger – preserved in the Holy Scriptures! Why is that? I think it is because God understands us and he appreciates it more when we are honest about what we truly feel, rather than when we deny our feelings. When we come to him admitting how angry we are and even reaching the point where we utter really angry words to express our emotions, we are humbled but at the same time encouraged that there is one who understands what we feel.

C. S. Lewis thought that the people who uttered the imprecatory prayers in the Psalms were sinning. Some scholars do not think so. We don't really know, though, for only God can see our hearts. It is he who sees our inmost thoughts. If those writers were indeed sinning when they uttered those prayers, however, then it is amazing that their prayers would even be allowed to be preserved in the Holy Scriptures! The content of these prayers can be shocking for some. But I think what this tells us is that we have a God who understands what we are going through. He allows us to struggle. As we have learned in the previous chapter, it's OK to struggle. What's more, he even allows us to be sinners – that is, he allows us to approach him even as sinners for that is what we are.

Let me be clear, though: I am not saying that he tolerates our remaining sinful or that he tolerates evil and sin. But the fact is that there are times when no matter how much we try, the lingering power of sin is still there. The problem arises when we are not allowed to admit to being sinners. We are not allowed to be sinners in the church. We pretend we are already OK when we actually are not. In some Christian communities, you are not allowed to be weak; you are not encouraged to show your anger. As a result, you feel alone. You feel guilty when you hear stories of people who love those who have treated them badly. But I would like to tell you that with the Lord you can be honest; you can be yourself and still be accepted.

But God also knows how difficult it is for us to be honest. Similar to when we are down, it is not easy to find the words to express our sorrow, our fear, or our anger. That is why the Lord provides us with the words in the Bible – we can pray these words. By providing us with words of prayer through the lament psalms, God challenges us to confront our own anger. And as we do, as we pray these imprecatory prayers, our anger begins to have a "name." Just like the experience of the writer in Psalm 57, when we are able to "name" our anger, we are able to somehow have control over it. When we know we are angry, then we can deal with it, first in the presence of the Lord.

As we pour out our hearts in honesty to God about what we feel, we also become aware of our own hearts. We realize we are not perfect, that we too are sinners. That is why after the psalmist uttered words of hate in Psalm 139:22, "I have nothing but hatred for them; I count them my enemies," he also prayed, "Search me, O God, and know my heart . . . See if there is any offensive way in me" (Ps 139:23–24). That's one of the good things about being true to the Lord: the eyes of our heart are able to see beyond our anger towards the person we hate. We become aware of our own heart, how we too are in need of God's mercy and grace. We experience a change within us.

In a number of the lament psalms we notice this change. We find this shift even in the most shocking imprecatory psalms in the Bible – psalms like Psalm 109. I think if there is such a thing as a psalm "for mature audiences only," this would be it. Just look at some of the prayer requests here:

> May his days be few; may another take his place of leadership.
> May his children be fatherless and his wife a widow.
> May his children be wandering beggars; may they be driven
>   from their ruined homes.
> May a creditor seize all he has; may strangers plunder the fruits
>   of his labor.
> May no one extend kindness to him or take pity on his
>   fatherless children.
> May his descendants be cut off, their names blotted out from
>   the next generation. (Ps 109:8–13)

These are some of the most appalling words in the Bible and that is why some do not advise including them in liturgical readings. Yet what we find at the end of this psalm is a change. We hear the following prayer:

> With my mouth I will greatly extol the LORD; in the great throng
> I will praise him. For he stands at the right hand of the needy one,
> to save his life from those who condemn him. (Ps 109:30–31)

By uttering this prayer and by being honest with God about what he feels, the psalmist feels at the end that there is someone who understands him, who feels what he feels: "For he stands at the right hand of the needy one" (Ps 109:31). We all need someone to listen to us when we are angry; but we also know very few people who can take our anger. The good news is that God can. When we are honest with him, humbly acknowledging before him how angry we are, we experience a change within us.

We find this change in another psalm, Psalm 28. Notice that in these verses the psalmist is uttering an imprecatory prayer, asking God to repay evil people for their deeds.

> Repay them for their deeds
>   and for their evil work;
> repay them for what their hands have done
>   and bring back upon them what they deserve.
> Since they show no regard for the works of the LORD
>   and what his hands have done,
> he will tear them down
>   and never build them up again. (Ps 28:4–5)

Then immediately in the next verses, we hear the following words:

> Praise be to the LORD,
>   for he has heard my cry for mercy . . .
> My heart leaps for joy
>   and I will give thanks to him in song. (Ps 28:6–7)

How can you move from cursing to praising after just one verse? How can you suddenly turn from being an angry person to become a praising person? I think we have here another demonstration of how expressing our anger before God can create a change within us. German scholar Heiler explains this change of mood in terms of a psychological change.[1] As we pour out our hearts to the Lord, something happens within us. Of course, it does not happen instantly. The verses in Psalm 28 may represent a long process of praying and being honest before God that the psalmist had to go through,

---

1. F. Heiler, *Prayer: A Study in the History and Psychology of Religion,* ed. and trans. Samuel McComb (London: Oxford University Press, 1932), 259.

before he could reach the stage where he could move from his anger to seeing the greatness of God and blessing him. As we pour out our anger to the Lord, our hearts are transformed and our eyes become clearer. We are able to see better and hopefully, are enabled to love our brother or sister in the process.

Praying for punishment?

But maybe some of you are saying, "That is easy for you to say because you have not experienced being a victim; you have not, for instance, lost a family member as the result of someone else's violence." It is one thing to pour out one's heart to the Lord in order to move from anger to love towards the other person; it is another to actually pray and wish that God would punish the wicked.

I remember watching a group of Christian leaders gathered for a prayer rally on TV. This was during the 2010 national election in the Philippines. One of the bishops was shouting as he prayed, "*Ibagsak Mo sila, Panginoon!*" ("Topple them down, O Lord!"). He was referring to corrupt candidates and government officials. These people of the government had done him no wrong personally, so the bishop was not really "processing" his anger. Rather, he was asking God to topple these corrupt leaders. Is it OK to pray this way?

The Bible actually contains prayers asking God to punish the wicked. In addition to the prayer of Psalm 28:4–5, we also find prayers similar to that of the bishop:

> Kill them not, lest my people forget; make them totter by your power and bring them down, O LORD, our shield! (Ps 59:11 ESV)

> Break the arm of the wicked and evil man; call him to account for his wickedness that would not be found out. (Ps 10:15)

> Surely God will bring you down to everlasting ruin: He will snatch you up and tear you from your tent; he will uproot you from the land of the living. (Ps 52:5)

We can feel Psalm 52:5 better in Filipino:

> *Ngunit ilulugmok ka ng Diyos magpakailanman, aagawin at hahatakin ka niya mula sa iyong tolda, at bubunutin ka niya sa lupain ng mga buháy.* (ABAB)

Again, like the prayers earlier, these words may be shocking to some. But the problem today is that we know only one type of prayer – blessing.

Even when our president and government officials are corrupt, for instance, we continue to pray for them to be blessed. I remember attending a prayer breakfast once at Malacañang Palace, where the president of the Philippines holds office. The president during this time was corrupt. But I noticed that when the time to pray came, all the prayers were positive; the prayers were all about blessings – bless the president, bless the cabinet members, bless the government. I am not saying we should not pray for God to bless our president and government. The problem comes when it is only this type of prayer that we know, when we continue to pray the same prayer over and over again without asking ourselves, "Is this still the right prayer for our particular situation?" Similar to our response towards tragedies, when we continue to sing happy songs even in the midst of suffering, we only know of prayers of blessing when it comes to our government.

Now please don't get me wrong. I am not inciting rebellion here. But it is much better to pray that God punish the wicked than to do it yourself. Rather than take the law into your own hands, go to the One who is righteous and just, and ask him to do something about the situation.

Do we really care?

On the flip side, continually praying for blessing even when there is so much corruption in the government may mean that we do not really care about what is happening. We do not care that the wicked continue in their wicked ways. We do not care about those who suffer as a result of their corruption. I think it is important that we pause and realize what we are really saying in our prayers. What we say to God in our prayers reflects our own beliefs – they shape our understanding and direct our forms of engagement. If we continue to pray that God will bless our government even when it is corrupt, then that tells us something about our own view of what is right. Some may say, "Why don't we just pray that God transform our corrupt leaders?" Well, praying that God bring them down is part of what it means for them to be transformed.

I think one reason why there is no change in our land is because we are not praying rightly: we tolerate the wrong – even perpetuating it and participating in it. This may also be the reason why the wicked and corrupt people around us, not just those in the government, do not fear God. No matter what they do, we still pray that God bless them. How fortunate they are indeed! I agree with what an official of the Commission on Elections told me – the reason why the government is not afraid of Christians is because we only pray for blessings; we are so nice. We do not know how to get angry.

The transformative value of anger

The value of the imprecatory prayers is that they not only assist us in the process of moving towards loving those who have done us wrong, but they also teach us the transformative value of anger. As theologian Beverly Wildung Harrison reminds us: "We must never lose touch with the fact that all serious moral activity, especially action for social change, takes its bearings from the rising power of human anger."[2] There is anger in the imprecatory prayers. You cannot read them without feeling their anger. When the psalmist prays, "Break the arm of the wicked" or "Bring them down!" he is not speaking softly. He is praying like the bishop, shouting, "*Ibagsak Mo sila, Panginoon!*" [Bring them down, O Lord]. And this may be one reason why some Christians do not like the imprecatory prayers. Praying the imprecatory psalms requires us to live a just life. It is hard to pray these prayers if we ourselves are practicing the very things we are praying against.

In order to appreciate the imprecatory psalms, we first need to understand who the wicked people being referred to are. Then we need to understand the situation of the people uttering these prayers. Earlier, I quoted from Psalms 52 and 10. From these two psalms, we understand that the wicked are those who:

1) are a "disgrace in the eyes of God" (Ps 52:1)
2) "practice deceit" (Ps 52:2); in Filipino terms they are "corrupt"
3) "love evil rather than good" (Ps 52:3)
4) "grow strong by destroying others" (Ps 53:7b)
5) take advantage of the poor – "in arrogance the wicked hotly pursue the poor" (Ps 10:2a ESV)
6) are boastful
   - He boasts about the cravings of his heart (Ps 10:3a)
   - "He says to himself, 'Nothing will shake me; I'll always be happy and never have trouble'" (Ps 10:6)
7) are greedy – "he blesses the greedy and reviles the LORD" (Ps 10:3)
   As I write this, military generals are being investigated for receiving money in the millions of pesos as "*pabaon*" (gifts). If this is true, then it is terrible that high-ranking officers can amass such

---

2. Whitehead and Whitehead, *Shadows of the Heart*, 47.

amounts of money while many of our soldiers suffer from lack of supplies and benefits. People can be wickedly greedy.

8) have no fear of God

- He "curses and renounces the LORD" (Ps 10:3b ESV)
- "In the pride of his face the wicked does not seek him; all his thoughts are, 'There is no God.'" (Ps 10:4 ESV)
- "His ways are always prosperous" (Ps 10:5a)

It's not that the wicked person is an atheist, but that he acts as if there is no God. He always gets away with being deceitful; he even becomes more prosperous. This is why he has no fear of God. How many well-known, influential people have been put in jail because of corruption? Not many, I'll bet.

9) murder the innocent

- "He lies in wait near the villages; from ambush he murders the innocent, watching in secret for his victims. He lies in wait like a lion in cover; he lies in wait to catch the helpless; he catches the helpless and drags them off in his net. His victims are crushed, they collapse; they fall under his strength." (Ps 10:8–10)

When I read these words I can't help but think about what happened in the province of Maguindanao on 23 November 2009. Fifty-seven people were brutally murdered, thirty of whom were reporters.[3] They had been accompanying the wife of a gubernatorial candidate who was on her way to file her husband's certificate of candidacy. This was big news, and thus it was being covered by those reporters. There were women among the victims, one of them pregnant. Who would have thought that they would all be killed? But the horrible, the unthinkable, happened. On that day, the Philippines gained the infamous record of having the greatest number of journalists killed in a single day. The murder had obviously been premeditated and was done without mercy. The killers buried the victims, some of them while still alive, for when the bodies were later pulled out of the ground, one woman's hand was still outstretched, indicating that she had been buried alive.

This is what the writers of the imprecatory prayers have in mind when they say, "Bring them down! Break the arm of the wicked!" These are the kinds of people against whom the imprecatory prayers are directed. Yes, we

---

3. The fifty-eighth victim has yet to be found.

are commanded to love others, especially our enemies. But the Bible also teaches us that God is just. And so these prayers should be understood within the realm of God's justice. We can understand how people can pray such prayers when members of their own families have been murdered.

I recently had the opportunity to teach in a town near the area in Maguindanao where the killings occurred. A student told of his experience in ministering to someone related to one of the victims. He had been leading a Bible study one night, sharing about forgiveness and love, when a young woman in the audience suddenly burst into tears. So he went to her and asked why – my student did not know that the lady was the daughter of one of those who had been massacred. How can you preach about love and forgiveness to this lady? There are no words to express the hurt and the pain.

A number of suspects have already been arrested and are now being tried in court for the massacre. One of them was the incumbent governor. No matter how the case turns out, the families of the victims know that nothing can bring back their loved ones. A reporter once asked the wife of one of those killed whether she had forgiven the perpetrators. She replied, "Even if I forgive them, I no longer have a husband who would come home and embrace me." She has been left with five children to support, and there were days when the children would come to her for food when she had none to give. Even if she forgives, she says, how can she raise five precious children on her own? No words can express such hurt and the pain.

It is still uncertain whether the victims and their families will ever get the justice they deserve. We often say that justice in the Philippines is "just-tiis" (the word "tiis" means "endure"). One of the prosecuting lawyers for the Maguindanao victims told me that, at the rate the case is going, it will take about a hundred years before a verdict is reached. The judicial system in our country can be hopeless. Situations such as this are one reason why the imprecatory prayers are important, for they offer hope to those who have suffered injustice. By crying out to God in their pain and agony, those who suffer can continue to put their hope in God – who promises that he will one day bring about true justice. It may not be in this life, but it will, for sure, happen in the next.

Exposing evil

Praying the imprecatory prayers exposes the evil and violence in our midst.[4] Violence is very real, happening not just in war-torn areas far away but also in our own neighborhoods. Its just that we don't want to talk about it – or maybe we just don't care because we ourselves are OK. I remember leading a Bible study for a group of British Christians. I was talking about these imprecatory prayers when one of them said, "I cannot understand how people can be so hurt and violated; how they can utter such harsh words."

Praying the imprecatory psalms makes us one with those who suffer. We give hope to those who are victims, and we expose the works of evil in our midst. What we have seen in the Psalms is how God's people process their anger in the presence of the Lord. They do not regard their experiences of sadness, fear, and anger as things alien to God's presence. It is these "negative" experiences that form the very subject and core of their conversations with God. The writers of the imprecatory psalms talk to God about how downcast they feel. They admit to him that they constantly tremble with fear. They admit their own struggles. They tell God how angry they are, how they feel about what their enemies have done to them, and what they really want in their hearts to happen to these people.

But what if the one you are angry with is God himself? Is it OK to be angry with God? Is it OK to question God? We will look at this in the next chapter.

---

4. Erich Zenger, *A God of Vengeance? Understanding the Psalms of Divine Wrath* (Louisville, KY: Westminster John Knox Press, 1996).

Encountering a psalm

Read Psalm 10.

- How do you usually handle your anger?
- Have you ever told God you are angry with someone? Have you tried praying for something bad to happen to that person? How do you feel about doing this? Do you think it's OK to express our anger to the Lord?
- How do you feel about praying that God bring down wicked or corrupt government officials (e.g. Ps 10:15: "Break the arm of the wicked")? Do you think as Christians we should be seriously praying for this in our churches?
- Are you angry with someone right now? The suggestion in this chapter is to express your anger to the Lord. Take this time just to open up your heart to the Lord. Tell him what you really feel about the person who has hurt you. You may want to write this in a journal or diary.
- Jesus commanded us to love our enemies. How do we reconcile this with the prayers of imprecations in the psalms?
- How do you preach the imprecatory psalms? Or do you preach them at all?
- What message(s) can we draw from the imprecatory psalms? Can you cite situations where these kinds of passages may speak powerfully?

9

It's OK to Question God

If God is almighty and good, why didn't he intervene and save my father from dying? My father was a good and righteous man!"

The woman was crying, almost shouting, as she spoke. This was during the funeral service for her father. Most of the people who were present were believers, and there was silence as they listened to her. Most of these Christians were stunned. They were used to hearing talk about God's goodness – "God is good all the time. All the time, God is good." To suddenly hear statements questioning the goodness and justice of God and his actions made them uncomfortable.

How do we respond to words of accusation directed at God? Is it OK to make statements like the ones this woman said? How do we handle it when our angry words are words actually coming from our own heart? Is it all right to be angry with God? Or if the words "angry with God" are too strong for you, is it wrong to feel bad about God? Is it OK to question him?

In the previous chapters I have tried to show that it's OK to be down, it's OK to be sad, and to cry; and it's also OK to be angry with others. Whatever our situation, we can bring it to God. We can tell him how downcast we feel and how angry we are with another person. We can lament about ourselves and about others before God. The question now is, "Can we lament against God?" I think this is the hardest dilemma. When struggling with ourselves and with those we hate, we can pour out our hearts to God. And when we are lonely and sad, we can also cry out to him. When treated unjustly by our enemies, we can be honest with him about what we feel. We can even pray that God punish the wicked. But if it is God himself whom we are complaining about, where then do we go? Do we complain to God against God? He is already the Supreme Court of all supreme courts!

In the olden days in Korea, many communities had a big drum called the *Shinmungo*, which means "the drum for hearing the cry for help of the people."[1] Anyone who was mistreated by his neighbors or by people in authority could beat the drum to call the attention of the king to what was happening and to ask him to do something about the situation. So whenever anyone experienced injustice of any sort, he or she would beat the drum to call the attention of the king. I wish we had such a drum here in the Philippines! But what if it was the king himself was the one being complained about? Could the early Koreans also beat the *Shinmungo* in that case? Similarly, can we express to God our laments and anger against him?

Lament against God in the Bible

Amazingly, what we find in the Bible is that people not only lamented about themselves and their enemies, they also lamented against God.[2] An example is Psalm 42/43. Here the psalmist:

- laments about himself: "Why are you downcast, O my soul? Why so disturbed within me?" (Ps 42:5)
- laments about his enemy: "Why must I go about mourning, oppressed by the enemy . . . my foes taunt me, saying to me all day long, 'Where is your God?'" (Ps 42:9b–10)
- laments to God against God: "I say to God my Rock, 'Why have you forgotten me?'" (Ps 42:9a). "You are God my stronghold. Why have you rejected me?" (Ps 43:2a).

What makes our God different is that even though he is the King of kings and the Lord of lords, he allows his people to express their honest questions to him. As we will see in the next section, Abraham pours out his heart to God when confronted with his continuing situation of childlessness. Moses argues with God's decision to destroy the Israelites. Habakkuk bangs on heaven's door with his fierce laments. Isaiah utters some of the most difficult words in the Bible. And Jeremiah questions God's absence, as did our Lord Jesus.

---

1. Chung-Choon Kim, "God's Suffering in Man's Struggle," in *Living Theology in Asia*, ed. John C. England (London: SCM, 1981), 17.

2. Claus Westermann, "The Complaint against God," in *God in the Fray: A Tribute to Walter Brueggemann*, ed. Tod Linafelt (Minneapolis, MN: Fortress Press, 1998), 238.

Abraham was honest with God about what he really felt

Have you ever had the experience of receiving a truly special promise? A good job offer with a high salary, a nice house, time with your family on a holiday somewhere, a present or gift for your birthday? Abraham received one of the most special of promises: God promised to give him many children. God even told Abraham that his descendants would be as numerous as the stars in the sky and the sand on the seashore. "If you can count these," he told Abraham, "then you can count your descendants." God's promise was very special because during that time, the more children you had, the more blessed you were understood to be. This may no longer be true today, of course, but for the people of Abraham's time, children brought security and the certainty of a good future. And so Abraham must have felt really excited about this.

But Abraham waited and waited, and nothing happened. He was not getting any younger; when the promise was given, he was already seventy-five years old. Waiting for something whose arrival has no promised date is torture! (Abraham had to wait twenty-five years from the time the promise was given before he finally had a son. And a specific date was given only in the twenty-fourth year!) You can imagine the frustration, the long months and years of waiting.

You may think of Abraham as one who was all-obedient and faithful. But there were times in his life when he felt like saying, "That's it. I can't take it anymore!" For him, having a son was everything. Even though he had become very rich (Gen 13:2), he was not happy. Even if was successful and experiencing victory over his enemies, all that was nothing to him if he had no son. That is why when God came to him one day and said, "Fear not, Abram, I am your *shield*; your reward shall be very great" (Gen 15:1 ESV), he said to the Lord, "O LORD God, what will you give me, for I continue childless, and the heir of my house is Eliezer of Damascus?" (Gen 15:2 ESV). I find this question of Abraham a bold one. It is bold because he was able to tell the Lord that he was not pleased, that he was not happy. He seemed to be telling God, "What is a shield to me? What are all these victories and riches to me without a son?" It's like those small *sarisari* stores in the Philippines that have this sign: "Credit is good, but we need cash."

How did God take Abraham's response? He could have rebuked him or scolded him for responding the way he did. He could have countered, "Do you know whom you're talking to? I am the God of the universe!" Amazingly, God did not rebuke Abraham or get angry with him. God knew and understood Abraham's struggle and frustration. He knew that Abraham was just being honest with him about what he was going through and what he felt about the whole thing. And God honors this kind of honesty. In fact, what we see next is God, instead of getting angry, assuring Abraham that he will have a son of his own, as well as lots of descendants (Gen 15:4–5). This tells us something about God's wisdom and patience: He allows his people to express their honest feelings and thoughts even though these may contradict what he tells them and wants them to know.

Moses argues with God

After the Lord brought the Israelites out of Egypt, he made a covenant with them. A covenant relationship is like marriage; it involves commitment and sacrifice. God initiated this covenant, reaching out to the Israelites and saving them, inviting them to be his people. But just as God promised to do certain things for the people, so there were also things that he required from them in order for them to be truly his. These are what we know as the Ten Commandments (Exod 20). All the Israelites agreed to obey the commandments and keep the covenant (Exod 24:7).

Among the first of these commandments is to not have any other gods besides the Lord. Unfortunately, after a short period of time the Israelites violated their commitment. Impatient and fearful because Moses was taking too long on the mountain, they went to Aaron, Moses's brother, and asked him to make them gods who would go before them. They told Aaron, "As for this fellow Moses who brought us up out of Egypt, we don't know what has happened to him" (Exod 32:1). Notice how they describe Moses here as the one "who brought us up out of Egypt."

Shockingly, Aaron did not hinder the people or rebuke them for thinking about making idols. He simply followed. Out of the gold from the people's necklaces and earrings, Aaron fashioned a golden calf. The people shouted, "These are your gods, O Israel, who brought you up out of Egypt" (v. 4). Here, they are saying that it's the golden calf – and not Moses – who brought them out of Egypt.

All this time, Moses was on the mountain with the Lord. He did not know what was happening back at the Israelite camp. But God knew, and he was angry. He interrupted his time with Moses and told him to go down because, as he said, "your people, *whom you brought up out of Egypt*, have become corrupt" (Exod 32:7). Notice how the Lord echoes the very words that the people had been saying about Moses. This is a change from what God had said earlier in Exodus 20:2: "I am the LORD your God, *who brought you out of the land of Egypt*" (ESV).[3] It seems like God was telling Moses: "They are not my people, they are your people. I don't want to have anything to do with them. Anyway, they are calling you as the one who brought them out of Egypt, not me." So angry was the Lord that he told Moses, "Now leave me alone so that my anger may burn against them and that I may destroy them" (Exod 32:10). This reminds me of Jesus's words to Peter, though used in a different situation: "Get thee behind me, Satan" (Matt 16:23 KJV).

Imagine God telling you to step aside. Would you stand in the way of the Lord? Yet Moses was not willing to allow God to destroy the people. Even when the Lord gave him an attractive offer that after he destroyed the Israelites, he would make Moses into a great nation (Exod 32:10) – Moses did not step aside. He even argued with God. Repeating the now popular phrase, Moses said, "LORD, why should your anger burn against your people, *whom you brought out of Egypt* with great power and a mighty hand?" (Exod 32:11). The Israelites had said earlier that it was Moses who brought them out from the land of Egypt (Exod 32:1). Then later, they ascribed this act of deliverance to the golden calf – "these are your gods, Israel, who brought you up out of Egypt" (v. 4). In his anger, God then called the Israelites "your (referring to Moses) people, whom you brought up out of the land of Egypt" (v. 7).

The credit for freeing the Israelites has now become like a basketball, which Moses passes back to God – where he believes it should be. But the way he does it is by quoting from God's earlier statement in Exodus 20:2 and then adding the words "with great power and a mighty hand." By adding these words, missing in the earlier occurrences of the phrase, "who brought you up out of the land of Egypt" (vv. 1, 4, 7),[4] Moses was telling God, "Lord, it's not me, and it's definitely not the golden calf; it's you. Only you can deliver us with such power."

After "correcting" God's statement, Moses questioned the wisdom of God's action: "Why should your anger burn against your people . . . Why should the Egyptians say, 'It was with evil intent that he brought them out,

---

3. The words in Exodus 20:2 and 32:7 only differ slightly, with the use of the verb "brought out" in Exodus 20 and "brought up" in Exodus 32. But the meaning is similar.

4. There is also a small but significant change of verb in v. 11. Instead of the verb "brought up" (vv. 1, 4, 7), Moses uses the word "brought out" in v. 11 – exactly the same word used in Exodus 20:2. These two words have similar meaning but are two different words in Hebrew. And I think the change is deliberate to make a point.

to kill them in the mountains and to wipe them off the face of the earth?'
Turn from your fierce anger; relent and do not bring disaster on your people"
(Exod 32:11–12). Notice that twice he asks God "Why?" (The question
"why?" is a characteristic feature of the lament psalms.) Moses was actually
asking God, "What will the other people say if you destroy the Israelites? Why
should they say that you brought them out of Egypt just to destroy them in
the mountains?"

And so Moses pleads, "relent and do not bring disaster on your people."
In the end, he asks God to remember his covenant with their fathers (v. 13).[5]
Amazingly, God "relented." Verse 14 tells us that "the LORD relented and did
not bring on his people the disaster he had threatened." Wow! Not only does
God allow his people to reason with him, question him, and argue with him,
he even allows them to win!

God doesn't want "Yes Lord, yes Lord" Christians

The wonderful thing is that with our God we have a voice; our opinion
matters. What we feel is important to him. This is because to God, we are
special. He does not see us as slaves but considers us his covenant partners.
Jesus tells his disciples, "I no longer call you servants . . . Instead, I have called
you friends" (John 15:15). Because God views us highly, he listens to us. God
does not want followers who are only "yes" people. The Lord does not seek
disciples who are only "Yes Lord, yes Lord" Christians. He wants covenant
partners who are able to express what they think and feel.

I know this is not easy for many of us who have come from a culture that
highly values respect for the elderly. In the Philippines we use the terms of
respect "*po*" and "*opo*" whenever we talk to the elderly. You don't question
an older person, much less God. We can take this kind of deference to the
extremes, however, to the point that the authority of the elderly becomes
absolute. Even when we know they are wrong, for instance, we just bow to
them. (Of course, we can also go to the other extreme where even a small
child can address his grandfather as "John." Some young people today no
longer have respect for elderly people.)

I remember growing up in an educational system where teachers were
the authority. You just never questioned them or challenged their position. So

---

5. The word "relent" in Hebrew can also be translated "change one's mind, repent,
be sorry."

even if I sometimes knew the answer to a teacher's question, I would be afraid to stand up and answer it. This became even more true when I had a question about the lesson or didn't agree with the teacher. It was unheard of to even consider addressing the teacher in a manner that would seem to threaten his or her authority. At home, my parents were sometimes so busy that they did not stop to listen when I tried to talk with them. (This has changed through the years, as we became more open with each other and I felt more valued.) Because of this, there were numerous times while I was growing up when I felt that my views and opinions did not matter. *Why speak?* Authorities were there to be respected at all times, and questioning them undermined their authority. So I did not question them at all.

That is why this story of Moses standing before God and being allowed to argue with him and speak his mind is really liberating and encouraging for me. Before this God, I feel empowered. I am valued. I have a voice. And you, too, have a voice. You can tell him what you think and he will listen.

A modern lament against God

I remember one incident of national concern. Our then-president had turned his office into a casino. We heard rumours of a midnight cabinet where political favors were handed out between shots of hard liquor, as well as confirmed reports of corruption at the highest levels of government. An impeachment case was filed on charges of bribery, betrayal of public trust, graft and corrupt practices, and violation of the Constitution. The whole nation was glued to television sets as events unfolded. It was better than any soap opera we knew of. I watched the proceedings on live TV with more intensity than when I watched a championship basketball game.

In one particular incident, the contents of an envelope were said to offer proof that the President was involved in corruption. There was heated debate about the legality of opening this envelope. In the end, the Senate voted whether the envelope should be opened (a "yes" vote) or not (a "no" vote). Unfortunately, the "no" vote won. And I was furious. I wanted to shout at the senators who had voted "no." I felt so angry that this had been allowed to take place.

We had a chapel service in the seminary the following day. I led the prayer and I used the prayers of lament as my guide, for I felt that the lament psalms expressed what we were experiencing and feeling at that time. We poured out our hearts to the Lord. As I led the prayer, I asked him, "Why are you allowing wickedness to reign in our land? Why did you allow the 'no votes' to win?" I pleaded for his mercy and grace, for him to act and do something in our land. I did not end the prayer on a positive note, but with a question directed to God.

What happened the following day was the making of Philippine history. All roads led to EDSA, the place where the People Power Revolution had occurred in 1986. People flocked towards the EDSA Shrine for a second People Power movement, calling on the president to step down. Over the next few days, the president was ousted and we had a new government. Looking back, that succeeding government also did not deliver as we had hoped. And things are not good even at present. But I have realized that when we, the people of God, gather and express our questions to him, he listens. He allows our honest questions and laments. The experience was indeed empowering. We, as God's people, can actively engage with God regarding matters of justice and righteousness in our land. As we have learned in the previous chapter, we can pray that God bring down the wicked. So we can express our honest laments to God, just like what the prophet Habakkuk did.

Habakkuk bangs on heaven's door with his laments

The prophet Habakkuk hurled some painful laments at God. Habakkuk could no longer bear the violence and injustices around him, and so he banged on heaven's door: "How long, O LORD, must I call for help, but you do not listen? Or cry out to you, 'Violence!' but you do not save? Why do you make me look at injustice? Why do you tolerate wrong? Destruction and violence are before me; there is strife, and conflict abounds" (Hab 1:2–3). Just like with Abraham, the Lord neither rebuked nor ignored Habakkuk. Instead, the Lord answered and initiated a series of dialogues between himself and his prophet. He told Habakkuk that he was doing something to effect the change he was asking for – he was raising up the Babylonians as his instrument to implement the change. This change was a welcome development for Habakkuk; it was the instrument for the change that he had a big problem with. How could God use the Babylonians, when they should be the first ones who should be destroyed? It didn't make sense to Habakkuk, to say the least. And so a series of laments – fiercer than the first – followed God's response.

> O LORD, you have appointed them to execute judgment . . . Your eyes are too pure to look on evil; you cannot tolerate wrong. Why then do you tolerate the treacherous? Why are you silent while

the wicked swallow up those more righteous than themselves?
(Hab 1:12–17)

God responds by telling Habakkuk that a solution will certainly come. For the meantime, he asks Habakkuk to wait for the appointed time (Hab 2:2–4). Habakkuk obeys; he waits and submits to God. Finally, at the end of the book we hear Habakkuk uttering the famous words of praise and confidence:

> Though the fig tree does not bud
>> and there are no grapes on the vines,
> though the olive crop fails
>> and the fields produce no food,
> though there are no sheep in the pen
>> and no cattle in the stalls,
> yet I will rejoice in the LORD,
>> I will be joyful in God my Savior.
> The Sovereign LORD is my strength;
>> he makes my feet like the feet of a deer,
>> he enables me to go on the heights. (Hab 3:17–19)

What was happening here? What had caused the change from lament to praise? What we have here is a long process that involved the prophet's wrestling in his own heart and with his God. He had to confront his situation and the fact that God seemed to be doing nothing. Then he needed to open his heart to God and tell him what was really in there, just like what Abraham did. It was only then that change occurred.

To speak of change, however, is to speak first of inner change. As Habakkuk poured out his heart to the Lord, his ill feelings about God, reflected in his laments, find an embrace. For the first time, Habakkuk felt that he was not alone. He realized that what concerned him was also a matter of great importance to the Lord. What is more, as Habakkuk became honest with God about what he saw as God's inaction, he experienced a deeper sense of intimacy with him, one that he had never had before. God had become to him not only a God when everything was OK; but also when things were not OK with the world and between himself and his God.

Honesty brings intimacy

It's the same with other relationships: The more open we are with a person about what we truly feel and think, the more vulnerable we become. But also, the more opportunity we have to be closer to the person with whom we are opening up. This is probably one reason why the honesty of the lament psalms is not common in the prayers of Christians today. Many just want a "casual" relationship with God, a relationship that is shallow and empty. But for those desiring to be deeper in God, there is no other way than to be genuine and honest. As we say in one of our Filipino proverbs: "*Ang nagsasabi ng tapat, nagsasama nang maluwat*" [The one who is honest about what he/she truly feels will keep his/her relationships intact].

Unless Christians today learn to be honest before God, they will not grow deeper in their relationship with him. Ultimately, the goal of this kind of prayer is intimacy with God. Some of our questions may never find their answers on this side of eternity. The woman I referred to at the beginning of this chapter may never, in her earthly life, be able to reach a place where she can say that she finally understands. But by opening up her heart to God, by honestly pouring out her questions and anger towards God, she will be drawn closer to him.

The book of Habakkuk ends without the promised deliverance. When Habakkuk penned his famous hymn of praise, nothing about his situation had changed; but something had happened in his heart – he had become closer to God. Unfortunately, Christians miss out on this important process that had taken place between God and his prophet, simply because we have tended to focus only on the last part of the book, ignoring the laments in the earlier parts. I think the words of praise at the end can only be understood properly when we read them in the context of Habakkuk's earlier laments. What we find in the prophet's experience is that not only does God allow his people to pour out their laments directly to him and not only does he respond to them, but he also uses these as a way to strengthen his people's faith. Without active engagement with God, there will not be any breakthrough in our relationship with him. It is those closest to God who are most honest with him – those like Jeremiah, Isaiah, and Jesus himself.

Jeremiah's bitter lament

Jeremiah's lament to God is more direct:

> You who are the hope of Israel,
>   its Savior in times of distress,
> why are you like a stranger in the land,
>   like a traveler who stays only a night?

> Why are you like a man taken by surprise,
>   like a warrior powerless to save?
> You are among us, O LORD,
>   and we bear your name;
>   do not forsake us! (Jer 14:8–9)

Isaiah's accusing lament

> Why, LORD, do you make us wander from your ways
>   and harden our hearts so we do not revere you?
> Return for the sake of your servants,
>   the tribes that are your inheritance. (Isa 63:17)

The logic of this prayer goes something like this: Because of their sins, the people have experienced the judgment of God and are now suffering. But actually, so the prayer argues, if God had not allowed their hearts to be hardened in the first place, they would not have rebelled against him and would not have been punished. Indeed, a prayer like this is hard to understand. But so is Jesus's own cry of abandonment.

Jesus's cry of abandonment

> My God, my God, why have you forsaken me?
>   Why are you so far from saving me, so far from the words
>   of my groaning? (Ps 22:1 ESV)

Jesus's prayer here is important for Christians because there will always be those who will say, "But these kinds of prayer are only in the Old Testament!" Well, here we have a prayer that not only comes from the New Testament, it also comes from our Lord himself. What is more, Jesus actually quotes this from the Psalms; and in doing so, he affirms the other prayers of lament in the Psalms. In fact, some scholars believe Jesus was praying through the lament psalms during his time of suffering.[6] This tells us how important the psalms of lament are when we go through times of extreme difficulty.

Another important lesson we learn from Jesus's prayer is that questioning God does not mean one is no longer submitting to God. We have to bear

---

6. William L. Holladay, *The Psalms through Three Thousand Years* (Minneapolis, MN: Fortress Press, 1993), 347.

in mind that prior to his uttering his cry of abandonment on the cross, Jesus had already prayed, "Not my will but your will be done." He was in total submission to his Father. Even on the cross, he affirmed his submission and his trust in his Father when he prayed, "Into your hands I commit my spirit." On the other hand, by praying Psalm 22:1, by crying out, "My God, my God, why have you forsaken me?" Jesus shows that the inverse is also true – that submission to God does not mean we can no longer ask questions, that we can no longer question him. We still can. We can submit to his will and question him at the same time. Thus, to the question "Is it OK to question God?" we say yes.

Not all questions are acceptable to him

Having said all this, it is now important to stress that not all questions and laments directed to God are acceptable to him. For instance, God condemned the murmurings of the Israelites in the desert. Many of his people were actually killed as a result (see Num 11:1–4, 33). God does find some questions directed to him offensive, such as those recorded in the book of Malachi:

> Another thing you do: You flood the LORD's altar with tears. You weep and wail because he no longer pays attention to your offerings or accepts them with pleasure from your hands. You ask, "Why?" It is because the LORD is acting as the witness between you and the wife of your youth, because you have broken faith with her, though she is your partner, the wife of your marriage covenant . . . You have wearied the LORD with your words. "How have we wearied him?" you ask. By saying, "All who do evil are good in the eyes of the LORD, and he is pleased with them" or "Where is the God of justice?" (Mal 2:13–17)

How do we know if our questions or manner of questioning is acceptable or not? There are really no hard and fast rules, for the line separating the highest levels of spirituality and blasphemy is filament thin.[7]

But first of all, I think we need to remember that this type of praying is not usual for Christians, or at least, I hope we do not pray like this all the time. The kinds of prayer we've seen arose out of experiences of constant exposure to pain and suffering. Or as writer Belden Lane explains, they "can result only

---

7. Belden C. Lane, "Hutzpa K'Lapei Shamaya: A Christian Response to the Jewish Tradition of Arguing with God," *Journal of Ecumenical Studies* 23, no. 4 (Fall, 1986): 567.

from a prolonged and painful look on unrelieved suffering."[8] Second, these prayers occur within the context of a growing relationship between God and believers. Those praying are simply being honest about what they really feel about God. They understand that in order to preserve their relationship and cause it to grow deeper, they have to be honest with the Lord. Honesty and genuineness before God is the key. As the Christian philosopher Kierkegaard says, "The most important thing is to be honest towards God."[9]

When we feel that what is happening is unfair and unjust, we can express this to the Lord. As Christian leader and Old Testament scholar Chris Wright says:

> In the wake of something like the tsunami . . . I am not ashamed to feel and express my anger and lament. I am not embarrassed to shed tears watching the news or worshipping in church after such terrible tragedies have struck again. I tell God I know and love and trust, but don't always understand, that I just can't get my head around the pain of seeing such unspeakable destruction and death. I will cry out on behalf of the wretched of the earth, "Why those poor people, Lord, yet again? Haven't they suffered enough of this world's gross unfairness already?"[10]

But what if after all that we have done, lamenting to God and all, still nothing happens? What do we do when everything fails? Is there room for failure in the presence of God?

---

8. Ibid., 584.

9. Cited in Abraham Joshua Heschel, *A Passion for Truth* (New York: Farrar, Straus and Giroux, 1973), 251.

10. Wright, *The God I Don't Understand*, 54.

Encountering a psalm

Read Psalm 22.

- Jesus himself prayed Psalm 22. Have you ever felt abandoned by God? Is it OK to be angry with God?
- How do you pray when you learn of many people dying in a war, of children dying of hunger, or of destruction in the wake of a tsunami?
- The road to intimacy with God is honesty. Do you have questions for God that you have been afraid to ask him because he might reject you? If so, write these down. Now come to God in prayer and be honest with him about your questions and how you feel.
- In a culture that highly values respect and the role of the elderly, how do you preach on these psalms that express questions to God? Is it OK to question God?
- How would you explain the lament in Psalm 22:1 and the fact that Jesus himself quoted from this psalm?
- What message(s) can we derive from the psalms that express laments against God?

10

It's OK to Fail

P astor, please pray for me. I will be taking a nursing exam next week," Zeny told me at the end of our worship service. Zeny (not her real name) was one of the members in my church. She spoke softly, making sure no one heard her. At the end of our brief meeting, she said, "Pastor, please don't tell anyone that I'm taking the nursing exam, and that I asked you to pray for me." Then she left. I wondered, *Why doesn't she want anyone to know that she's taking the exam?* We normally tell others our prayer requests.

Weeks later, I learned that Zeny had failed the exam. One of our church members informed me about this. But Zeny never spoke to me about it. Maybe she was ashamed to approach me or to talk about what had happened. I don't know. But when someone confronted her and asked her whether she had taken the exam, Zeny denied it. Maybe this was the reason why she did not want others to know – Zeny was afraid that if she failed and that if others knew she had asked for prayer, that she might be put on the spot. Others would think that her faith was weak. So Zeny just hid it all. On the other hand, I'm sure that had she passed the exam, she would have stood in front of the church and testified about it, and the whole congregation would have rejoiced with her. Because she failed, however, she went through the experience alone. There was nothing to celebrate, nothing to talk about.

A seminary professor shared a similar situation with me. Two members of his church had also taken a nursing exam. The Sunday before the exam, their whole church had prayed for them. Unfortunately, only one passed. When the next Sunday came, the pastor announced the good news: One of their members had passed the exam! Everyone praised God for the answered prayer, but nothing was said about the one who had failed. There was complete silence about it during the entire worship service. No one talked to the nursing student who had failed. What, after all, could they say?

It's difficult isn't it? If you were one of the members, how would you have responded? If you were the pastor, how would you have handled this? What would you say? Would you dare to say anything at all?

We don't know how to respond to failure

The difficulty is that in many of our churches today, we do not know how to deal with cases like this. Similar to when Christians experience disaster or calamity, we do not know how to respond when a fellow believer experiences failure. Many times, we are quick to rationalize. We reason that God has a purpose. Or maybe that there is something wrong with our sister – that that's the reason why she failed – she needs to repent of some sin. But I think another reason is that we are not really open to accepting defeat or failure. We emphasize victory and success so much that we no longer want to talk about defeats or failures. So we hide them instead. Or worse, like Zeny, we even lie about it. In the church it is *not* OK to fail.

Someone once tried to publish "the testimony of a woman who did not receive a healing that was prophesied for her." He thought it would be fair to publish such a case at least this one instance, to show that not everyone actually gets healed. But his request was turned down.[1]

Some churches emphasize the positive so much that they are not willing to look at reality anymore. There is a strong pressure to always end in a victorious, positive way. It's sad. Because there is no room in the church for unanswered prayers or for experiences of defeat, Christians are sometimes forced to hide or tell a lie. We can celebrate easily; we know perfectly how to do that. But we do not know how to mourn with those who are defeated. In addition, those who fail can themselves be quick to rationalize their experience and say, "God has his own purpose." Maybe, but that does not erase the pain that one feels as a result of failure. Zeny had tried her best to prepare for the exam. I'm sure she had prayed hard about it. *Why did I fail?* she must have wondered. And yet, she suffered the pain of her failure alone.

Space for failure

As we have learned from the previous chapter, we can come to God and pour out our heart to him, even asking him, in Zeny's case, why he did not allow

---

1. Ellington, "The Costly Loss of Testimony," 53.

her to pass the exam. He invites us to come to him and openly share our pain with him – not hide it. The many lament psalms testify that God does indeed welcome the honest expression of whatever we feel. There is place in the presence of God for our questions. There is space for our failures in his presence.

I wish this were true in our churches. I wish there was space in the church for our failures. I wish there was a place where I could be allowed to be broken, where I would not need to hide if I failed. I know I will never find a perfect church or community in this world, and that such a place exists only in heaven. But I also believe that the church, being the Body of Christ, is called to be such a place, or at least a reflection of such – a place where we can cry, where we do not need to hide because we have failed, a place where we are accepted even when our prayers remain unanswered. A place where we know people can be with us not only when we are victorious, but also when we do not succeed – to listen to us, cry with us, or simply be with us in our times of sadness. Then there will be no need to keep our prayer requests to ourselves or to be ashamed when our prayers are not answered. There will be no need to limit our testimonies to testimonies of victories and success. Our prayers, too, will not be limited to praise and thanksgiving; there will be space for our questions, our silences, and our uncertainties as well.

This is my wish, my dream. I know this is also the dream of many Christians who are suffering either with defeat or failure. Maybe you, too, have been wishing for a long time to create a space in the church for our negative experiences. I share this dream with you and pray that one day, even if only through a glimpse, that the Lord will allow his church to experience what being a real community means.

Psalm of darkness

Psalm 88 is one of the darkest psalms. So dark is the psalm that it actually ends with the word "darkness" in the original Hebrew. There is no movement to praise in Psalm 88. Some Christians will not be comfortable with this psalm. They want to move to praise right away. But life is not always like that.

Some people in the church today cannot find an end to their sufferings. They try and try, but they just cannot get up. They cannot see any light at the end of the tunnel. Like the writer of Psalm 88, they lament and never get to experience praise – not even a respite. They find themselves in darkness no matter what they do. They cry, but always, no one seems to be listening. The church, unfortunately, is sometimes not a good place to be in when you are experiencing Psalm 88. People there would tell you that you cannot be in darkness for a long time if you are a true believer. That maybe there is sin within you or that you are not in the center of God's will.

Well, maybe they're correct; some people going through dark times do have sin or issues that they need to settle before God and others. That may be why they are experiencing darkness. But this is not true for everyone. At least, it wasn't true for the writer of Psalm 88. There is nothing in the text to suggest that the psalmist was being punished for his sin. This was also not true for St John of the Cross, the writer of the famous book, *The Dark Night of the Soul*. The fact is that some believers will go through times of darkness in their lives, times when they will feel alone, rejected by their friends, and even by God himself.

I have experienced darkness many times. In one of my journal entries I wrote:

> This morning as I woke up, there is such heaviness words cannot describe. I feel empty, hopeless. I even had a nightmare last night and when I woke up, I could still feel its effect. I don't know what to do. There's really nothing about this day or any day, for that matter, that excites me. Everything is just plain blue and stark dark. I can't breathe.

Do you know what helped me during my times of darkness? Psalm 88. In this psalm, I felt for the first time that I was not alone. People before me, including God's precious people, have gone through some really dark times. What's more, I found the very words written in Psalm 88 resonating with my own experience. In one of my lowest moments – even my friend in the USA who was talking with me over the phone could sense the heaviness in my heart – I found the words of Psalm 88:4 especially encouraging: "I am like a man without strength." The word "man" in Hebrew can also be translated "strong man." This guy is supposed to be a strong man and yet he acknowledges that he feels so weak. He is supposed to be victorious and strong but he admits, "I do not have the strength." Well, I already had my PhD. My dissertation had been published by a prestigious publisher less than a year after I had received my PhD. And yet, in spite of this, I felt so weak. "Weak" is even too weak a word to describe my state. What I felt was more like helplessness. I felt like I could not even lift my head to see whether there was somebody there to help me, or open my eyes to see if there was any light left. In Psalm 88, however, I found the strength I needed to open my heart to God and just whisper: "I am like a man without strength. Lord, I can no longer carry on. Please help me."

Maybe you feel like that right now. Maybe you have just gone through a terrible failure, and you feel like your whole life is a mess. You feel like a disposable cup, used up a hundred times. The comforting thing about this dark psalm is that, at least, the psalmist can cry. The mere fact that he is crying out to God means he still believes there is Someone listening to him even though he also feels that that Someone has let him down. Here the hope lies not in the answer but in the question. In the midst of all his pain and suffering the psalmist shouts, "But I cry to you."

In other psalms, the word "But" at the beginning of statements often signals a change to some form of resolution or thanksgiving, or a declaration of trust (Ps 55:23; Ps 13:5 "But I trust in you"). Here in Psalm 88, there is no such change to praise or resolution. But I think this psalm is actually a statement of trust. In times of darkness, the equivalent of "But I trust in you" is "But I cry to you." Even when we no longer have the strength to carry on, we can at least cry to someone. You too can cry. While it is true that we draw strength on our journey from God's answers and encouragement, we also know of times when we draw our strength from our very weakness.

What we need in our weakness

Many of us feel weak. When you look at people in the church, many of them look OK. But deep inside, many are struggling with broken lives. A successful person in the church may appear to have it all together in the eyes of others. Many may not be aware, however, of how much this person struggles, even with just how to live another day – what he or she may see as another day of pain, defeat; each day seemingly a lie.

You look at certain people and they look OK. But look at their marriage; all damaged, with the commitment to stay together being the only thing that's left. You look at people with certain jobs and you envy them, wishing you were like them – clever, smart, sociable, gifted. But you do not know how insecure they are deep within – the insecurity may be the reason why they keep trying to stay on top, for that may be the only thing that gives them a reason to live. Take that away from them, and what's left would be emptiness like that of a deep well with no water.

The last thing we need is another sermon telling us that everything will be OK if only we will believe, if only our faith is strong. The last thing we need is for someone to tell us that everything will be OK. What we do need is the assurance that what we are experiencing is not abnormal, that we are not beyond the bounds of God's gracious care. That even our defeats still find a place in God's sovereign and gracious care. This assurance is important especially during the times when our churches conduct themselves in a triumphalist manner. This can be seen in our sermons – we seldom hear sermons on lament, if we even get to hear them in church at all. Unfortunately, many of those who do teach lament end up highlighting only one side, the element of praise, by always stressing the need to end on a positive note. I once heard a pastor preach over a podcast, "Lament *must* turn to praise." This view of the lament psalms stems from a particular perspective – the one-sided understanding that any expression of the lament *must* emphasize the element of praise.

Lament to praise only?

When I was doing my research on the lament psalms for my PhD, I was struck by the way many scholars tended to read the lament psalms through the lens of the lament-to-praise movement. So strong is this view that some scholars will even go to the extent of changing the text, so that it will read more positively.

For instance, Psalm 9/10 actually moves from thanksgiving to lament. In Hebrew, Psalm 9/10 is a single psalm, composed using the Hebrew acrostic. Verses 1 and 2 of Psalm 9 begin with the first letter of the Hebrew alphabet, verse 3 with the next Hebrew letter, and so on until we reach the end of Psalm 10, which begins with the last letter of the Hebrew alphabet (Ps 10:17).[2]

Now, the first half of the psalm (Ps 9) is mostly thanksgiving. It would actually form a perfect example of a thanksgiving psalm. The problem is that, in the middle of the psalm, the mood suddenly changes to lament. How can thanksgiving turn to lament? This has baffled many scholars. So one scholar suggested that it was the use of the Hebrew alphabet that was responsible for

---

2. I have discussed the following psalms in my article, "Preaching Lament," in *Reclaiming the Old Testament for Christian Preaching*, eds. Grenville J. R. Kent, Paul J. Kissling, and Laurence A. Turner (Downers Grove, IL: IVP Academic, 2010), 64–84.

the movement to lament.[3] He argued that by the time he got to the start of Psalm 10, the composer was already at letter "l" of the Hebrew alphabet. This forced him to begin the verse with the word *lamah*, which in English means "Why?" Thus, the verse reads, "Why, O LORD, do you stand far off? Why do you hide yourself in times of trouble?" (Ps 10:1).

But of course, if the intention of the author of Psalm 9/10 was to continue with thanksgiving, he could have easily done so. He could have used other Hebrew words beginning with the Hebrew letter "l." Unfortunately, some scholars have one-sidedly emphasized the lament-to-praise movement in the lament psalms, thus failing to see what is actually there.

Fortunately, the people who composed the Psalms were more realistic than many scholars and pastors today. Believers of old knew that life is not monolithic; it does not consist of only one form. As they knew from experience, the life of faith can turn from praise to lament. The amazing thing is that, as we have learned in the previous chapter, the writers were willing to struggle with God with their questions, pour out their hearts to him, and even storm heaven with their "Whys?" But equally helpful, I think, is their particular view of life – it is a view that allows for experiences of defeat. Even though the writers continually asked God why they were facing defeat and so on, they at least recognized their experiences for what they were. In their language of faith, the writers had a category called defeat or failure, and it was this that enabled them to recognize what they were going through when they came to God.

The believers of old were also more open to experiences of ambiguity and uncertainty, as reflected in another lament psalm, Psalm 12. This psalm begins with lament, with the writer crying out to God for help because "the godly are no more" (v. 1). In the middle of this cry for help, God responds in the most direct way possible. God speaks, "I will now arise" (v. 5). The psalmist couldn't have asked for more – God had already spoken.

How we wish that in our prayers, we would also hear the Lord speaking directly to us. Notice how in the next verses, there is a change to a confident mood: "And the words of the LORD are flawless, like silver refined in a furnace of clay, purified seven times. O LORD, you will keep us safe and protect us from such people forever" (vv. 6–7). Psalm 12 could have ended on a high note with verse 7: "O LORD, you will keep us safe and protect us

---

3. The great German scholar Hermann Gunkel made this suggestion in his Psalms commentary.

from such people forever." But no, the psalm ends with the following words: "On every side the wicked prowl, as vileness is exalted among the children of man" (v. 8 ESV). Again, some scholars find this rather anticlimactic, so they try to manipulate the text, suggesting some changes in it. But the text as it stands reads plainly – the wicked are still very much active. Actually, they are more active than ever.[4] Even if some scholars do not like the ending, I think what makes this psalm attractive even though it is anticlimactic is that we can actually see our lived realities in it.

I remember Marvin, an American PhD student whose story reflects the movement of Psalm 12. Marvin and his wife had been struggling financially, moving often over a six-month period because they struggled with paying rent. One day, Marvin's wife came home with good news – she had found a job at a place nearby, and she could start right away. The couple was really happy. Like Psalm 12, their lament had turned to praise. Marvin's wife went to work the following day while he continued with his research. Later that day, however, his wife came home and told Marvin that the salary that went with the new job was not what they had been expecting; it was way too little. The couple found themselves back in lament.

We can find similar stories in every field of life. A student begins his college studies, and the following years are a time of stress and lament both for him and his parents. His mother and father sacrifice a lot to pay his tuition, while he works hard to fulfill all the requirements. After four or five years of this, the student graduates. This calls for celebration! He and his family are moved to praise. But after graduation, this student has difficulty finding a good job. The jobs available are not related to what he had been trained for. In the end, he is forced to settle for less; what's available is better than nothing. This story is common in the Philippines, and it is even worse among those who remain jobless for years after graduation.

The reality is that things do not always turn out as we expect. Even when we have already received assurance that our prayers will be answered, ambiguity remains. We think we have everything covered. We have prayed hard. We have felt God's presence. We know we are precisely in the place where God wants us to be. And yet, like the writer of Psalm 12, we find ourselves confronted with the same problems or even more challenging situations. Our circumstances are not different from those of the believers of old.

---

4. I have discussed Psalm 12 in more detail in my book, *The 'Uncertainty of a Hearing': A Study of the Sudden Change of Mood in the Psalms of Lament* (Leiden: Brill, 2008).

The question is: Are we willing to accept that? Again, some may say, "Well, that's in the Old Testament. With the coming of Jesus, there is no more defeat. Christ suffered so we might have a victorious life." But actually, if we look at the New Testament, particularly Romans 7, we encounter the same perspective on the life of faith – one that accommodates experiences of struggle and defeat even in the Christian life, this time on moral grounds.

Struggle in the New Testament

In Romans 7 Paul confesses: "So I find this law at work: When I want to do good, evil is right there with me. For in my inner being I delight in God's law; but I see another law at work in the members of my body, waging war against the law of my mind and making me a prisoner of the law of sin at work within my members" (Rom 7:21–23).

Some scholars argue that here, Paul is either talking about his experience before he became a believer, or about somebody else's experience.[5] But as we can see in the verses, the statements have been constructed using the first-person singular "I," indicating that Paul himself is the one speaking. The verbs used are in the present tense, which means Paul is talking about his present experiences, not things of the past. The "I" voice is also present in the whole of verses 14–25. Further on, Paul's description, "in my inner being I delight in God's law" (v. 21), cannot be said of one who still does not know the Lord. Besides, in Romans 5–8, Paul is dealing with the subject of the Christian life. All these lead us to the conclusion that the apostle is talking about his own experience – which is ongoing – or that he at least includes himself in the experience he is talking about. Of course, Paul also goes on to speak of the Christian life as one of "no more condemnation" (Rom 8:1). But the latter does not alter the reality presented in Romans 7.

The image of a "prisoner" in verse 23 speaks powerfully of a defeat: ". . . making me a prisoner of the law of sin . . ." This situation leads Paul to utter a cry of lament similar to that of Psalm 12: "What a wretched man I am! Who will rescue me from this body of death?" (Rom 7:24). Like in Psalm 12, we also find a movement to praise in the next verse: "Thanks be to God – through Jesus Christ our Lord!" (Rom 7:25a). But then, also like Psalm 12, Romans 7

---

5. The arguments that Paul is here speaking as a believer are clearly set out in Anders Nygren, *Commentary on Romans* (Philadelphia, PA: Fortress Press, 1949); C. E. B. Cranfield, *Romans: A Shorter Commentary* (Edinburgh: T & T Clark, 1985); James D. G. Dunn, *Romans 1–8* vol. 38A, WBC (Dallas, TX: Word Books, 1988).

ends with the sober reality of the continuing presence of struggle and defeat in the life of the Christian: "So then, I myself in my mind am a slave to God's law, but in the sinful nature a slave to the law of sin" (Rom 7:25b). While Paul acknowledges that he is a slave of God, he also acknowledges that he is a slave to the law of sin.

Thus, it is clear that Christians still do experience defeat. Becoming a Christian does not mean a complete release from all struggle and defeat. As New Testament scholar James Dunn explains, "Paul can and does readily conceive of believers being frequently defeated (v. 23) in the continuous sequence of moral choices which confront them (6:12–23)."[6] In saying this, we are not giving excuses for moral lapses, we are only acknowledging that defeat is still part of the life of faith. The encouraging thing is that as we accept our realities of defeat in the light of God's mercy and grace, we are changed. To quote the words of Buckley:

> We cross the bridge back into a world filled with loss and failure, a land scarred by sin and injury. We leave behind fantasies of perfectionism and of friendships that never change. If the world we reenter is impermanent, it is also inhabited by forgiveness. This is not a place of hatred or resentment, of bitterness or revenge. On this side of the bridge our negative emotions become our allies helping us face the dangers and reconciliations that mark our path.[7]

In this world we can never cross the bridge and come to a side where everything will be OK, where there will be no defeat. But at least we can cross the bridge as a different person, more open to change, more open to pain, because we have learned to share our pain and defeats with God and with others.

---

6. Dunn, *Romans 1–8*, 412.

7. Cited in Whitehead and Whitehead, *Shadows of the Heart*, 28.

Encountering a psalm

Read Psalm 88.

- In this chapter I related the experience of two believers taking the same exam. The church prayed for them, but only one passed. How do you deal with situations like this, especially if you are a pastor?
- We have learned that even people close to God experience the "dark night of the soul." Looking at your own walk with God, have there been times when you also suffered through this experience? How do you deal with failure or defeat?
- What images, words, or phrases in Psalm 88 resonate with your own experience during your dark moments? Using these images/ words/phrases, silently come to the Lord in prayer.
- Do you know of someone who is going through his or her own darkness? Bring this person to the Lord as you pray the words of Psalm 88. You could even offer to pray Psalm 88 with him or her.
- How do you make room for experiences of failures in your preaching?
- What does a psalm like Psalm 88, which contains no movement to praise, have to tell us about the life of faith?
- Do you think it is all right to end a worship service with a question or an absence of closure, instead of on a positive note?

11

Conclusion

When I first submitted the initial drafts of this book to my editor, he asked me how I intended to end the book. The subjects in this book can be heavy and dark. Not being OK. Sadness. Crying. Fear. Struggles. Being angry. Questioning God. Failures. It would be good to end with some assurance and hope.

Looking back, I realize that the hope is the lament itself. For centuries, great thinkers, theologians, and philosophers have tried to resolve the question of suffering. I think one answer to suffering is lament. The lamenting is in itself a sign of hope. We may never find a solution to our individual suffering or to the sufferings of this world. But God has provided us, in the lament, a way of coping with our sufferings. Somebody once sent me this text message: "An umbrella cannot stop the rain, but it allows us to stand in the rain." Lament cannot solve all our problems. But it can create the needed space where we can deal with our sufferings.

The lament, however, is not just a coping tool. It can become a means of growing in our intimacy with God. By being open to God about our own brokenness and about the real condition of our hearts, we place ourselves in his loving embrace. We no longer have to hide our pain; we can actually bring it to the Lord. We don't have to be afraid of getting rejected for our failures; we are already accepted, loved, and cherished as we are. There is room for our questions, struggles, pain, and failures.

Some may consider lamenting a sign of weak faith. But actually, it is an act of faith. We lament because we believe there is someone listening. In the lament, we encounter a God who cannot be swayed by our pious talk and unreal assumptions. He is a God who can be touched by a broken soul, a soul that is real and not covering up, a soul that simply says, "O God, darkness is my only companion."

I went through a lot of darkness myself during the writing of this book. Many times I asked the Lord, "How can I write this book when I am like this – struggling, lonely, depressed?" There were times when I thought of changing the title of this book, for it doesn't feel good to be NOT OK. It is painful, difficult, tormenting, and agonizing. But the Lord allows us to go through the darkness so that we may reach out to those who are also in darkness. The good news is that we do not need to be completely OK to be able to minister to others. For spiritual director Henri Nouwen, "the crucial question is not, 'How can we hide our wounds?' so we don't have to be embarrassed but 'How can we put our woundedness *in the service of others?*"[1] For we know that "only the bruised, wounded minister can powerfully connect with those who are badly wounded."[2]

Are you wounded? Do you feel tired? Do you feel empty? Do you feel excluded because you are suffering? Do you feel as if you are the only person who is lonely and sad in the world? Do you feel like crying this very moment?

Someone is listening. Someone can feel what you feel. Someone understands. You do not have to express your praise or words of trust when you feel like shouting or blaming someone. You do not have to force yourself to be OK if you are not. It's OK to be not OK.

---

1. Quoted in Wil Hernandez, *Henri Nouwen*, 116.
2. Ibid.

Appendix

Sample Sermons on Lament Psalms[1]

In the opening chapters of this book, I stated that we had to do certain things when preparing to preach on the psalms of lament:

1. Pay attention to the movement between lament and praise in these psalms.

2. Identify the types of suffering depicted in each psalm.

3. Discern what messages about God, the life of faith and reality in general we can derive from the depictions of sufferings.

4. Participate in each lament psalm by actually praying the words of the psalm, experiencing the movements between lament and praise yourself, and bringing your own experiences and that of others to God as you identify with the sufferings depicted in the psalm.

Now that you have finished the book, you will have a far better idea of what those instructions mean. So let us now try to apply them to particular psalms and give you some examples of how to go about developing a sermon on a lament psalm.

Psalm 12

Psalm 12 is a good place to start because it contains verses that explain what lament is. The lament psalm is a cry "from the depths" of suffering, uttered or addressed to God.

---

1. Unless otherwise indicated, the Scripture version used in the Appendix is ESV.

1.   What is the movement in Psalm 12?

In Psalm 12 we can discern a movement from lament (vv. 1–4) to certainty (praise) (vv. 6–7). In the middle of the psalm we find an explicit response from Yahweh, which explains the shift to the element of assurance in verses 6–7. But in spite of this divine response, the psalm returns to lament at the end. The words of certainty and assurance are followed by a statement that basically expresses the same concern that the psalmist had at the beginning: "On every side the wicked prowl."

2.   What experiences of suffering are depicted in the movement?

The psalmist may be suffering as a result of wicked people's oppressive acts (vv. 1–4). But reading the overall movement in the psalm adds another dimension to his suffering – he is suffering in spite of the fact that God supposedly has already answered him. This brings up the whole question of the presence of wickedness in a world supposedly controlled by God. This leads us to the next question.

3.   What message(s) about God, the life of faith and reality in general can we derive from these experiences?

The experience of suffering reflected in Psalm 12 teaches us that there are times when the element of tension persists even with the divine response.

4.   Experiencing Psalm 12

Pray the words of the psalm. Specifically, we may ask, "What particular experiences of suffering in the lives of others or in our own life are similar to that expressed in the psalm?" One possible example could be the experience of pursuing a degree. We lament our way through our studies and move to praise as we successfully complete the degree. But then the uncertainties of securing a job after the study can be so daunting that we find ourselves again back in the situation of lament.

Sermon outline on Psalm 12 "Return to Lament"

A. The movement in the lament: from lament to praise then back to lament
   1. From lament (vv. 1–4)
      a. Cry for help (v. 1)
         - "Help!" (v. 1)
      b. Arising out of suffering (vv. 1–4)
         Life when there are no more godly people around:
         - Lies (v. 2)
         - Pride (v. 3)
         - Oppression (v. 4; cf. v. 5)
      c. Addressed to God
         - "Help, O Lord!" (v. 1)
         - "May the Lord cut off all flattering lips" (v. 3)
   2. To praise (vv. 5–7)
      a. The divine response (v. 5)
      b. Assurance resulting from the divine response (vv. 6–7)
   3. Back to lament (v. 8)
      a. The lament at the beginning: "The godly are no more" (v. 1 NIV)
      b. The situation at the end: "On every side the wicked prowl . . ." (v. 8)

B. The psalmist's experience of suffering
   1. Life when there are no more godly people around (vv. 1–4)
   2. Uncertainty in spite of the divine response (v. 8)

C. The message of the psalm
   1. The life of faith: tension and ambiguity remain
   2. God: divine inscrutability

Conclusion: There are times when uncertainty remains even in the midst of our certainties. But through it all, the encouraging thing is that we have a God to whom we can cry even in the midst of the tensions of the life of faith.

Contexts matter

As you can see from the example above, the main thing about preparing a sermon on the lament psalms is the interplay between lament and praise within a psalm. These movements reflect the experiences of the people and contain messages about the life of faith. But in addition to this, we also need to consider the surrounding contexts of the psalm we are considering. Recent studies show that there is deliberateness in the arrangement of some psalms. The psalms were not arbitrarily put together; there is some order in the way they were put together. This does not apply to every psalm. But it is a good practice to consider context of the preceding and following psalms. Further, we also need to consider what the NT is saying about our text, especially if the psalm is quoted or alluded to in the NT. In our sample sermon on Psalm 22 below, we demonstrate how considerations of both the surrounding context and that of the NT contribute towards the making of the sermon.

In the sample sermons below, the first part follows the guidelines on how to prepare the sermon while the second part is the actual outline of the sermon.

Psalm 22

For preparing the sermon, we try to answer the following questions:

1. *What is the overall movement in Psalm 22 in terms of lament and praise?*

    Read the whole psalm. As can be observed, the psalm is almost equally distributed between lament and praise. The first half is lament (vv. 1–21); the second half is praise (vv. 22–31). But unlike the other psalms containing the movement from lament to praise (e.g. Ps 13) the two sections in Psalm 22 are juxtaposed, preserving the element of tension between lament and praise within the whole composition.

    The juxtaposition of lament and praise in Psalm 22 highlights the sense of contradiction felt by the psalmist. This is reflected further in the prayer. The psalmist complains that unlike his fathers, who were delivered and heard when they called to the Lord (vv. 4–5), he did not receive an answer (v. 2). The context of the surrounding psalms further brings out the element of tension in

Psalm 22. Psalm 22 is preceded by two psalms which emphasize the truth that God answers prayer. In Psalm 20 the people prayed for their king: "May the Lord answer you . . ." In the following psalm – Psalm 21 – the king rejoices because of the answer to the prayer. In contrast to this, the psalmist cries out in Psalm 22, "My God, I call to you by day, but you do not answer" (22:2). The following psalm – Psalm 23 – which is a psalm of trust further brings out the contrast between Psalm 22 and its surrounding context.

2.   *What experiences of suffering are depicted in the movement?*
The juxtaposition between lament and praise, observed above, reflects the suffering experienced by the psalmist. The psalmist felt really down, viewing himself as "a worm and not a man" (v. 6). He felt abandoned by God himself (v. 1). He was so close to God, calling him "my God." He even claims, "from my mother's womb you have been my God" (v. 10). Thus, to be left without an answer brought about feelings of hurt within him. In Filipino terms, we would call this *"pagtatampo"* – a feeling of hurt resulting from a failure on the part of someone really close to you to fulfill that which is expected of him/her. In the case of the psalmist, he was expecting God to deliver him because of his covenant relationship with him. But this did not transpire. As a result, he felt hurt. The good thing was that he did not contain within him what he felt but expressed this to the Lord.

3.   *What message(s) about God, the life of faith and reality in general can we derive from these experiences?*
The psalm reminds us of the reality of tension in the life of faith. We may liken the two halves of the psalm (lament and praise) to the cross and resurrection, respectively. Although Jesus was already resurrected, all of us have yet to experience the reality of this truth. Presently, we are in between. We are a people of the cross at one and the same time. This is the overall shape of our life with God. There will be times when the answer we hope to receive will not come; when instead of answer, there will only be frustrations and even persecutions. How then do we live in the face of this reality? Psalm 22 provides us with a guide in living in the midst of the tensions of life.

Title: "My God, my God, why have you forsaken me?" Living in the Midst of the Tensions of the Life of Faith

Text: Psalm 22
Outline:

Introduction

A. Tension in the Life of Faith
1.   There are times when we're strong and there are times when we feel like a worm
    a)   The same David who declared: "For by you I can run against a troop, and by my God I can leap over a wall" (Ps 18:29) also said, "I am a worm and not a man" (22:6)
2.   While some received the answer to their prayers, others didn't
    a)   Context of Psalm 20–21 highlights the fact that God answers prayer
        i)   Psalm 20 represents the prayer of the people for their king: "May the Lord answer you in the day of trouble!" (v. 1)
        ii) Psalm 21 expresses the joy of the king in having the prayers answered (v. 1)
    b)   In contrast to the above, David complains, "O my God, I cry by day, but you do not answer" (22:2)
    c)   While his forefathers were delivered when they cried for help (22:3–5), he received no answer (22:2; cf. 22:6–8)
3.   Our life is marked by both lament and praise (this is reflected in the overall structure of Ps 22)
    a)   Lament (vv. 1–21)
    b)   Praise (vv. 22–31)
4.   Even Jesus prayed Psalm 22
    a)   Matthew 27:46
5.   Application: what experiences of tension are you going through right now?

B. Living in the Midst of the Tensions
1.   Accepting the fact that our life consists of both lament and praise
2.   Making lament part of our prayer
    a)   by becoming more honest to God about:
        i)   what we feel towards him (vv. 1–2)

ii) what we are going through and what we feel about it (vv. 3–8)

b) by pleading for God's deliverance

i) description of situation (vv. 6–8, 12–18)

ii) petition (vv. 11, 19–21)

3. Making praise part of our prayer

a) by testifying to others what God has done (v. 22)

b) by exhorting others to praise the Lord (vv. 23–26)

c) by extending God's praise to the ends of the earth and for the coming generations (vv. 27–31)

Conclusion: Here the preacher may ask the whole congregation to read the whole psalm. The reading may be divided into two parts – lament and praise, verses 1–21 and verses 22–31, respectively. At the end of the first part, ask the congregation to bring to the Lord their laments, if any. At the end of the second half, let the congregation bring to the Lord their praises.

Superscriptions matter

Another thing to consider is the superscription to each psalm, that is, the short notes before the first verse of every psalm. Those who put the Psalter together added the superscriptions some time after the psalms were written. They thus represent a particular way of looking at the psalms. The superscriptions as it were provide windows into how the people of old interpreted the psalms. A close consideration of these superscriptions, especially those with brief historical background, can be a good resource for developing sermons on the Psalms (see Ps 57 below).

Psalm 57

1. *What is the overall movement in Psalm 57 in terms of lament and praise?*

    Psalm 57 contains an overall movement from lament (vv. 1–6) to praise (vv. 7–11). It begins with a cry for mercy (vv. 1–2) followed by an expression of confidence that God will answer his prayer (v. 3). The psalm continues the lament by describing the situation (vv. 4, 6). In between the lament in verses 4 and 6 there is a refrain which is repeated later (v. 5; cf. v. 11). The psalm is actually like a modern song with two stanzas (vv. 1–4 and vv. 6–10), with the refrain after each stanza (vv. 5 and 11). But even though the refrain occurs twice, its meaning differs. The first one is more of an assertion of trust in the midst of the lament while the second is the praise proper.

2. *What experiences of suffering are depicted in the movement?*
The contrast between the sections containing lament and praise reveal a very difficult situation on the part of David. The language "my heart is steadfast" (v. 7) brings out the element of uncertainty which characterized the experience of David in the first part. Verse 1 talks about "storms of destruction" (note: the word "storms" is in the plural. The passage is not talking about a simple storm of life, but a serious or dangerous one). See also the description in verse 4: "My soul is in the midst of lions." Like in the case of the "storms" we are not to take the "lions" here literally. But we can sense the element of danger in the poetic language. Thus, while there is singing in the second part of the psalm (v. 7b), there is crying and pleading for mercy at the first section (v. 1). All of these make Psalm 57 a good psalm for people going through dangerous situations and other occasions where one feels helpless.

The superscription further provides us with a picture of the situation out of which David finds himself. The whole superscription reads: "To the choirmaster: according to Do Not Destroy. A Miktam of David, when he fled from Saul, in the cave." This indicates that this psalm was used for singing. The words "according to do not destroy" may refer to the tune of the psalm. Though this is uncertain, a tune called "do not destroy" sounds dangerous enough. Then we are given a brief historical note on the situation of David – he was fleeing from Saul.

As noted above, the superscription can be valuable for preparing a sermon on the lament, especially those with historical background like Psalm 57. There are about thirteen of these in the Psalms. A closer examination of these shows most of them talk about a very difficult time in the life of David – fleeing from his son Absalom (Ps 3); feigning madness for fear of his life (Ps 34); and in one of the lowest points of his spiritual life, committing adultery with Bathsheba (Ps 51):

Psalm 3:1 A Psalm of David, when he fled from Absalom his son.

Psalm 34:1 A Psalm of David, when he feigned madness before Abimelech, so that he drove him out, and he went away.

Psalm 51:1 To the choirmaster. A Psalm of David, when Nathan the prophet came to him, after he had gone in to Bathsheba.

It is not the David who is successful and victorious, but the David who is struggling, running for his life, in danger, that is highlighted in these superscriptions. Why is this so? One possible explanation is that it is these which resonate with the experiences of the believers of old.

3. *What message(s) about God, the life of faith and reality in general can we derive from these experiences?*

Psalm 57 reminds us of the difficulties that mark the life of God's people. We often find ourselves in situations which are way beyond what we are able to overcome by our own strength. At the same time, the experience of David and the way he dealt with it as reflected in his prayer gives us a guide in terms of how we can also navigate our own way towards restoration.

Title: "Be exalted, O God, above the heavens." Experiencing God through the Storms of Life

Text: Psalm 57

Outline:

Introduction

A. The "storms" in the life of David
   1. The situation as depicted in the superscriptions in Psalm 57 and other psalms with brief historical background (e.g. Pss 3 and 51; see above)
   2. The twice-repeated prayer, "be merciful to me" (v. 1), indicates the situation confronting David is serious indeed

3. The phrase "storms of destruction"[2]
   a) The phrase speaks of a very dangerous situation
   b) Note the plural form of the noun "storms"
4. The description of his enemies as "lions," "fiery beasts" (v. 4; cf. v. 6)

B. The "storms" in our life today
   1. "Storms" in our country, both literal and figurative
   2. "Storms" in our churches
   3. "Storms" in our families and personal lives

C. How David faced his "storms" and what we can learn from it
   1. David humbled himself before God
      a) He asked for mercy (v. 1a)
   2. David trusted in God
      a) He took refuge in God (v. 1b)
      b) One of the most common titles attributed to God in the Psalms is "refuge" or rock
      c) Reason: Because people often find themselves in trouble
   3. David cried out to God
      a) Yes, even a macho man like David cries too
      b) And he cries a lot
         i) Psalm 3:4 – To the LORD I cry aloud, and he answers me from his holy hill.
         ii) Psalm 5:2 – Listen to my cry for help, my King and my God, for to you I pray.
         iii) Psalm 6:9 – The LORD has heard my cry for mercy; the LORD accepts my prayer
         iv) Psalm 22:2 – O my God, I cry out by day, but you do not answer, by night, and am not silent
   4. David faced his fears
      a) He took the courage of "naming" his fears
      b) The use of imagery in verses 4 and 6 is a way of giving a name to his fears and struggles
         (Some people think that admitting our fears is a sign of weakness. But it is actually a sign of faith when we are able to face our issues and confront them. It certainly takes a lot of

---

2. This is comparable to what Paul is talking about when he mentions the "day of evil" (Eph 6:13). We do experience difficult situations. But there are days when the attack is downright fierce.

courage to do that. Psychologists tell us how crucial it is that we name our fears or sufferings. By doing so we are able to weaken the grip of our fears.)

5. After David did the above, he:
   a) was able to sing, "Be exalted O God, above the heavens" (v. 5)
   b) received assurance (v. 7)
   c) praised the Lord (vv. 8–10)
      If earlier he was in lament, now he is in praise. He has moved from lament to praise.

6. But remember, David experienced this because:
   a) He first cried out to God
   b) He took refuge in God
      (He was able to say, "my heart is steadfast" twice (v. 7) because he also cried twice "have mercy on me, O God, have mercy on me.")
   c) He faced his fears

Conclusion: The road that leads to restoration is through lament. Without lament our praise will be empty. As Mays puts it:

If praise does not contain the memory of needs that have been met, hurt healed, sorrow comforted, loneliness visited, of life instead of death, then praise loses its theme and reality . . . We need to read through its prayers on the way to its hymns. There has been a tendency in the church's use of the Psalter to employ only or primarily the hymns, but if we go to the joyous hymns and the psalms of trust only and too quickly, we will never know the true power and purpose of the hymns.[3]

---

3. Mays, *Preaching and Teaching the Psalms*, 26.

Further Reading

Billman, Kathleen D., and Daniel L. Migliore. *Rachel's Cry: Prayer of Lament and Rebirth of Hope*. Eugene, OR: Wipf & Stock, 1999.

Bradbury, Paul. *Sowing in Tears: How to Lament in a Church of Praise*. Cambridge: Grove, 2007.

Brueggemann, Walter. *The Message of the Psalms: A Theological Commentary*. Minneapolis, MN: Augsburg, 1984.

Mays, James L. *Preaching and Teaching the Psalms*. Louisville, KY: Westminster John Knox, 2006.

McCann, J. Clinton, and James C. Howell. *Preaching the Psalms*. Nashville, TN: Abingdon, 2001.

Villanueva, Federico. *Lamentations: A Pastoral and Contextual Commentary*. Carlisle, UK: Langham Global Library, 2016.

Langham Literature and its imprints are a ministry of Langham Partnership.

Langham Partnership is a global fellowship working in pursuit of the vision God entrusted to its founder John Stott –

to facilitate the growth of the church in maturity and Christ-likeness through raising the standards of biblical preaching and teaching.

Our vision is to see churches in the majority world equipped for mission and growing to maturity in Christ through the ministry of pastors and leaders who believe, teach and live by the Word of God.

Our mission is to strengthen the ministry of the Word of God through:
• nurturing national movements for biblical preaching
• fostering the creation and distribution of evangelical literature
• enhancing evangelical theological education
especially in countries where churches are under-resourced.

Our ministry

Langham Preaching partners with national leaders to nurture indigenous biblical preaching movements for pastors and lay preachers all around the world. With the support of a team of trainers from many countries, a multi-level programme of seminars provides practical training, and is followed by a programme for training local facilitators. Local preachers' groups and national and regional networks ensure continuity and ongoing development, seeking to build vigorous movements committed to Bible exposition.

Langham Literature provides majority world preachers, scholars and seminary libraries with evangelical books and electronic resources through publishing and distribution, grants and discounts. The programme also fosters the creation of indigenous evangelical books in many languages, through writer's grants, strengthening local evangelical publishing houses, and investment in major regional literature projects, such as one volume Bible commentaries like *The Africa Bible Commentary* and *The South Asia Bible Commentary*.

Langham Scholars provides financial support for evangelical doctoral students from the majority world so that, when they return home, they may train pastors and other Christian leaders with sound, biblical and theological teaching. This programme equips those who equip others. Langham Scholars also works in partnership with majority world seminaries in strengthening evangelical theological education. A growing number of Langham Scholars study in high quality doctoral programmes in the majority world itself. As well as teaching the next generation of pastors, graduated Langham Scholars exercise significant influence through their writing and leadership.

To learn more about Langham Partnership and the work we do visit **langham.org**